PASSIONATE ATTACHMENTS

PASSIONATE ATTACHMENTS
Thinking About Love

EDITED BY
Willard Gaylin, M.D.
AND
Ethel Person, M.D.

THE FREE PRESS
A Division of Macmillan, Inc.
NEW YORK

Collier Macmillan Publishers
LONDON

The Free Press
A Division of Macmillan, Inc.
866 Third Avenue, New York, N.Y. 10022

Collier Macmillan Canada, Inc.

First Free Press Paperback Edition 1989

Printed in the United States of America

printing number

1 2 3 4 5 6 7 8 9 10

Library of Congress Cataloging-in-Publication Data
Passionate attachments.

   Bibliography: p.
   Includes index.
1. Love-Psychological aspects.   2. Interpersonal
relations.   3. Psychoanalysis.   I. Gaylin, Willard.
II. Person, Ethel Spector.
BF575.L8P36   1988   306.7   87-20185
ISBN 0-02-911431-4

Contents

Acknowledgments   *vii*

Introduction: Thinking About Love   *ix*
WILLARD GAYLIN and ETHEL PERSON

Editors and Contributors   *xiv*

1 *The Nature of Passionate Love*   *1*
MILTON VIEDERMAN, M.D.

2 *Passionate Attachments in the West in Historical Perspective*   *15*
LAWRENCE STONE

3 *Four Mischievous Theories of Sex: Demonic, Divine, Casual, and Nuisance*   *27*
WILLIAM F. MAY, PH.D.

4 *Love and the Limits of Individualism*   *41*
WILLARD GAYLIN, M.D.

5 *Between Conventionality and Aggression: The Boundaries of Passion*   *63*
OTTO F. KERNBERG, M.D.

6 *Two Cheers for Romance*   *85*
STANLEY CAVELL, PH.D.

7 *The Riddle of Femininity and the Psychology of Love*   *101*
CAROL GILLIGAN, PH.D. and EVE STERN

Epilogue
Passionate Attachments: The Essential
but Fragile Nature of Love   *115*
ROBERT MICHELS, M.D.

Notes   *123*

Index   *129*

Acknowledgments

Although academics have implicitly acknowledged the focal role of romantic love, they have displayed a profound reluctance to expose love to any rigorous examination. To overcome this reticence, the Columbia Psychoanalytic Center recently brought together a group of humanists from different fields (the topic of love being much too broad to be in the province of any one discipline alone) to start an interdisciplinary dialogue on the nature of love.

This interdisciplinary impulse, intrinsic to the philosophy of the Columbia Psychoanalytic Center, had also informed several earlier symposia, among them "The Fate of Individualism in Our Time: Narcissism and the Limits of Autonomy," and "Truth and Its Limits: Public and Private Domains."

The academic aversion to any serious dialogue on the subject of romantic love is perhaps reflected in the problem we had in funding the conference that dealt with it, a difficulty not confronted in the earlier ones. We are therefore particularly grateful to the Zalman Bernstein Foundation which showed no such prejudices and whose Board saw the merits of thinking (and talking) about love. The conference, under the auspices of the Columbia University Center for Psychoanalytic Training and Research and the Association for Psychoanalytic Medicine, took place on November 10, 1984. This book has evolved out of those discussions.

The editors wish to acknowledge the contributions of the other members of the Program Committee, Richard G. Druss and John Rosenberger, and of the Arrangements Committee as well: John Rosenberger, Lee Gardner, Robert A. Glick, Eric Marcus, and Howard Millman. We are of course grateful to our contributors who have been generous in their time and effort, and to our editor Erwin Glikes for his guidance and good humor. Joan Jackson, the administrator of the Columbia Center, and Doris Parker, its librarian, have given unstintingly of their time and energy; they have typed the manuscript and kept after us and have been instrumental in bringing together this volume. We also want to thank Dr. Fred Lane, past president of the Association for Psychoanalytic Medicine, and Dr. Robert Liebert, the current president, for their cooperation in co-sponsoring the symposium, and now the book.

Introduction
Thinking About Love

WILLARD GAYLIN AND ETHEL PERSON

As Glynn Issac said, love is a topic "which, in spite of its interests, has no experts—except insofar as we are all experts." We are drawn to explore love because as psychoanalysts we are aware of its extraordinary importance in the life of the individual; but we are also impelled by a certain shock at the curious neglect in the psychoanalytic literature of so fundamental a human experience—a point remarked upon, elaborated, and "explained" by several other contributors to this volume.

Of course psychoanalysts in their daily practice have been aware of the crucial role that loving and being loved play in the happiness and fulfillment of the individual patient, and the many miseries fostered in their absence. Despite this explicit acknowledgment of the focal role of romantic love in practice, there has been a pronounced reluctance to explore its theoretical aspects in any rigorous fashion.

Psychoanalysis is not alone in its attitude. Other disciplines in the biological and social sciences, including other psychologies, have also ignored the subject of love. Perhaps we are intimidated by a subject so critical yet so fundamentally subjective. How can one maintain rigorous standards, in an age of empiricism, with a subject that resolutely resists quantification, measurement, or objectification? Yet, the sexual revolution which was launched under the powerful impetus of Freud's work, and the reevaluation of gender role encouraged by the feminist movement, demand a new and careful consideration of the nature and meaning of romantic love. It is time for all of us in all the disciplines of human behavior to begin thinking about love—not "attachments," not "cathexis," not "object relations," not "fusions," nor "identifications"—but "love."

For psychoanalysts, the capacity to love has always been a leading component of our implicit, if not articulated, working definition of mental health. "Arbeit" and "liebe" have been tacit touchstones used by psychoanalysts in their everyday work. But what is "liebe"? The Freudian literature is sadly lacking in direct discussions of that love which Freud implicitly acknowledged as being of such fundamental importance to human satisfaction.

Freud dealt with love in many works, tangentially and anecdotally. In that confused, pessimistic, contradictory, and extraordinary masterpiece of his adult life, *Civilization and Its Discontents,* Freud considers the possibility that the only thing that may make sense out of the absurd condition of the existential world is human love. He was aware of both the difficulty of achieving love, and of the inherent pain in extending one's identification to others who are as vulnerable as one's self.

Freud, always the pessimist, was not sanguine in his appraisal of people's ability to achieve mature love. Part of his tragic vision stems from what he believed to be the inherent tendency toward the degradation of the love object and the inevitable ambivalence in any love relationship, in addition to the inherent difficulties of uniting the tender and sexual components due to unresolved oedipal conflicts. Nonetheless, Freud offered love as perhaps the one hope of comfort or meaning in a world of pain and confusion.

Freud's ambivalence toward the nature of romantic love is apparent throughout his work. Certainly in his developmental orientation he saw the capacity to subordinate one's primary interest in self to an involvement with a person of the opposite sex as the benchmark of a healthy and mature adult, a sign of having resolved the challenge of the Oedipus complex. Most analysts have followed this lead of Freud and have regarded love somewhat more optimistically than has the master himself. Even if not proponents of *passionate* love, they have endorsed affectionate "bonding" as a mature capacity and a reasonable life goal.

Yet Freud, dedicated anti-romanticist though he was, nonetheless was innately more romantic than many of his followers. He also depicted love as a restoration of the earlier blissful relationship between mother and child. Indeed, his final formulation of love emphasizes the projection of the ego-ideal onto the beloved. For the psychoanalysts who followed him, Freud set a normative standard by encouraging a developmental point of view in which both health and maturity were defined in terms of capacity to enjoy adult love.

Nonetheless, for the intellectual community at large, Freud was to bury love in his nineteenth century "materialist" attempt to reduce all emotionality to terms that might have been understandable in the laboratories of Helmholz and Wundt. Moreover, with the development of the libido theory Freud forced attention to the inner conflicts of the individual, thus deflecting primary consideration of the interpersonal relationships and their impact on the development of the self. In the process he reduced love to a sublimated aspect of libido. While he saw this sublimation as central to personality formation, its effect was catastrophic to an understanding of passion and emotion in general—and love in particular. Love now was simply the transformed energy of the driving sexual instinct. It is sex which is the central force, the vital element which propels all behavior. Love has been reduced to a derivative phenomenon.

Love, however, will not remain a subsidiary or secondary event, certainly not in this emerging post-modern phase when we begin to see a rebirth of romanticism in all areas of human intellectual life. Love *is* a central part of the human condition and demands direct and serious attention.

Yet not psychoanalysts alone, but sociologists, historians, and humanists have neglected love in their writings. Only the poets, the fiction writers, and the theologians have maintained the romantic tradition, and even the latter in their frantic haste to be "modern" and "socially relevant" have shied away from a central consideration of love. Who can blame the academician? How can one study something about whose very nature there seems little agreement?

There is one powerful tradition that argues that love is inherent in the human soul and psyche, that it is a given, not requiring any clarification, that it is a part of the genetic endowment of the human species. This tradition emphasizes the biological roots of community. It builds on that aspect which Freud said was the most powerful biological determinant on the developing human being—the prolonged dependency of the human child. The case has been made for a biological directive toward the family and for the attachment supporting the family structure. Those who support this theory see love as the product of the social evolution of a species that is an obligate social animal. They agree with Aristotle on the absolute imperative to maintain the view of Homo sapiens as a political and social animal.

In contrast some historians point to the cultural variability of love and take a totally different position. They argue that love—or at least romantic love—is learned, that it is not an essential part of human nature. They point out that our cultural sanction of love as a prelude to marriage is of relatively recent origin and therefore requires explanation.

Marriage was originally a legal contract designed to implement social necessities and provide a setting of stability for the raising of children. In society's upper echelons it was used to unite kingdoms, to cement alliances, and to exchange wealth and property. Only in the romantic traditions of the twelfth and thirteenth centuries was the concept of romantic love first fully developed, drawing its inspiration in part from Christian theology and in part from the Islamic Sufi tradition of mystical eroticism.

In this chivalric tradition, romantic love was only sustained through chaste and unfulfilled yearning. Only late in the Arthurian tradition of courtly love did marriage come to be seen as the end toward which love should strive. Some historians argue that it was not, indeed, until the nineteenth century—

with the widespread availability of the novel—that romance became a "sentimental love religion." And of course it can be argued that it is only in the West that romantic love has been fully developed as an ideal to be actually sought.

Nonetheless, romantic love has been reported in varied and diverse cultures in antiquity, in the bosom of the Church, in the popular niches of common culture.   •

Of course, the difficulty of talking about the nature of human love is simply one component of the difficulty of talking about the nature of human nature. We are unique and strange animals. Only with modern biology can we recognize how different we are from even our closest cousins, the apes and the monkeys. There is nothing in the current human condition that could have been anticipated from an examination of the species below us. That powerful and extraordinary phenomenon— the human imagination—is capable of transforming everything, as we psychoanalysts know only too well. Sources of pride can be seen as humiliating, subjects which normally support the ego can be seen as depleting it, victory can be turned into defeat, and that same defeat can be used as the material of a future victory. We are born without wings and we fly faster than the eagles. We plumb the depths of the oceans without gills. We transform even the nature of heredity. It is of the nature of human nature to change our nature. How then can we talk about that which is "natural"?

It is the powerful recognition of the transforming quality of the human imagination that makes libido theory with its model of animal instincts appear, once and for all, as too limiting, too confined, and too unimaginative a model to encompass human love. No, the libido theory is not the last word on love, nor is the literature of bonding drawn from animal experiments, nor is the literature of attachments drawn from developmental psychology. We must tackle—head-on—the subject of romantic love, recognizing that we may make little progress, but comforted by the knowledge that ultimately the most important questions to deal with are those that are essentially unanswerable. It is time to start thinking about love.

Editors and Contributors

Stanley Cavell, Ph.D., is Walter B. Cabot Professor of Aesthetics and the General Theory of Value, Harvard University.

Professor Cavell's work in the theory of knowledge and the philosophy of art is exemplified in his books *Must We Mean What We Say, The Senses of Walden, The Claim of Reason,* and *Pursuits of Happiness: The Hollywood Comedy of Remarriage.*

Willard Gaylin, M.D., is President and Co-founder of The Hastings Center; Training and Supervising Analyst, Columbia University for Psychoanalytic Training and Research; Clinical Professor of Psychiatry, Department of Psychiatry, College of Physicians and Surgeons, Columbia University.

In 1982 *The Killing of Bonnie Garland* by Dr. Gaylin was selected by *The New York Times* as one of their "Notable Books of the Year." Dr. Gaylin writes on psychiatry, ethics, law, and public policies. Other books include *Feelings: Our Vital Signs, The Rage within: Anger in Modern Life, Violence and the Politics of Research,* and *Rediscovering Love.*

Carol Gilligan, Ph.D., is Professor of Education, Harvard University.

Professor Gilligan won the Outstanding Book Award from the American Educational Research Association (1983) for her book *In a Difference Voice: Psychological Theory and Women's Development.*

Otto F. Kernberg, M.D., is Associate Chairman and Medical Director, The New York Hospital-Cornell Medical Center, Westchester Division; Professor of Psychiatry, Cornell University Medical College; Training and Supervising Analyst, Columbia University Center for Psychoanalytic Training and Research.

Dr. Kernberg is the author of *Internal World and External Reality: Object Relations Theory Applied, Borderline Conditions and Pathological Narcissism, Object Relations Theory and Clinical Psychoanalysis,* and *Severe Personality Disorders: Psychotherapeutic Strategies.*

William F. May, Ph.D., is Cary M. Maguire University Professor of Ethics, Southern Methodist University.

Professor May published most recently *The Physician's Covenant: Images of the Healer in Medical Ethics.* His next volume will deal with the patient's ordeal.

Robert Michels, M.D., is Barklie McKee Henry Professor and Chairman, Department of Psychiatry, Cornell University Medical College; Training and Supervising Analyst, Columbia University Center for Psychoanalytic Training and Research.

Dr. Michels is the author of more than 100 scientific articles, a member of several medical journal boards, including *Psychiatry* and the *Journal of the American Psychoanalytic Association,* and Chairman of the Editorial Board of the textbook, *Psychiatry.*

Ethel S. Person, M.D., is Director and Training and Supervising Analyst, Columbia University Center for Psychoanalytic Training and Research; Professor of Clinical Psychiatry, Department of Psychiatry, Columbia University College of Physicians and Surgeons.

Dr. Person's major professional interests include psychoanalytic and psychiatric education, the development of sexuality and gender, and the psychology of women. In 1981 she co-edited *Women—Sex and Sexuality* which received an Award for Excellence in the Field of Education by Chicago Women in Publishing. Her book, *Love in Our Time,* is scheduled for publication in 1988.

Eve Stern is a writer. She received a Mellon Fellowship in the Humanities in 1986.

Lawrence Stone is Dodge Professor of History, Director of the Shelby Cullom Davis Center for Historical Studies, Princeton University.

His books include *The Family, Sex and Marriage in England, 1500–1800,* and *An Open Elite? England 1540–1880.*

Milton Viederman, M.D., is Professor of Clinical Psychiatry, Cornell University Medical College; Training and Supervising Analyst, Columbia University Center for Psychoanalytic Training and Research.

Passionate Attachments

The Nature of Passionate Love

MILTON VIEDERMAN

Passionate love must be distinguished from its more restrained cousin, affectionate love, which often follows it and which, though not devoid of lust, is less dominated by its power and all-inclusiveness. Passion is an unstable or impermanent state, though to say this is in no way to devalue it or to view it necessarily as primitive. It is a state experienced only by some in their lifetime.

The psychoanalytic examination of passionate attachment is in itself a signal of the coming of age of one aspect of psychoanalysis: so far there have been remarkably few references to passion in psychoanalytic literature, although there are many references to love. There are reasons why passion may have been ignored. Passionate attachment is such an all-encompassing and global experience that it can be seen and felt only as a complete whole. Engel and Schmale have pointed out that one of the problems psychoanalysts have in defining patterns in the so-called "psychosomatic diseases" is that the analytic tool is so sensitive that it dissects to the point where the overall and distinguishing configurations disappear.[1] Similarly one cannot study cell structure in its broadest outlines with an electron microscope. This may be true of passionate love as well. In analyzing passionate love down to its component elements, one loses the qualities that make it specific and unique. One discovers elements that do not distinguish it from affectionate attachments and other broader areas of fantasy and experience.

My discussion will be in three parts. I will first examine the multiple definitions of the word "passion" to delineate the phenomenon. Second, I will review the psychoanalytic literature on passion. Finally, some of the attributes and dynamics of passionate attachment will be examined.

DEFINITIONS

The first definition of passion in the *Oxford English Dictionary* has to do with the suffering of pain (in particular the Passion of Christ on the cross), the suffering of martyrdom, and affliction generally.[2] This aspect of suffering clearly has pertinence to unrequited passionate love and is an aspect of many powerful erotic transferences in psychoanalysis that at least in part are motivated by the guilty need to suffer. In such situations the patient, choosing passionate attachment to the analyst even though aware that sexual satisfaction is impossible, experiences masochistic gratification unconsciously. A variant of this was observed in a patient (analyzed some years ago) who experienced guilt after a childhood sexual seduction. In adult life she developed a passionate attachment to a homosexual man and later a passionate erotic transference. Both situations permitted the experience of passionate excitement but inevitably the pleasure was coupled with the frustration of non-gratification, which alleviated her guilty need to suffer and to punish herself for what she had experienced as a childhood sexual transgression. In some situations, then, suffering may be closely related to passion.

A second set of definitions in the Dictionary, has to do with the idea of being acted on or afflicted by an external agency, which extends to "any kind of feeling by which the mind is powerfully affected or moved; a vehement, commanding or overpowering emotion including the wide array of feelings such as ambition, avarice, desire, hope, fear, love, hatred," etc. Here the emphasis is on uncontrollability, and spontaneous generation, with the sense that the power originates in the outside world rather than from within. It is to be noted that passionate love often is tinged or in some situations even dominated by any of the feelings delineated above, though the predominant conscious experience usually is related to desire, hope, love, etc. This definition emphasizes the intensity of feeling rather than its precise content.

The final category of definitions of passion is the one most closely associated with the subject of this volume. It relates to "amorous feelings; strong sexual affection; love; tender passion; sexual desire or impulse with the idea that an object is pursued with zeal."

At first glance these definitions seem to be radically different. Can one find a common denominator in comparing the passionate lover of women, the passionate lover of God, or the passionate ideologue bent on a search for Utopia? Yet similarities exist. Each is devoted to the object of his passion. Each would in some measure sacrifice himself for that object. As Robert Michels has pointed out, the object of passion becomes an essential and unifying theme for the person's life and defines not only his identity, but his world view.[3] Is it possible that in using the same word, we are actually identifying something that is more than superficial? Psychoanalytic theory lends itself readily to the view that the three phenomena in question may on one level reflect different modes and directness of expression of libidinal and aggressive drives. The religious ascetic who masochistically punishes his body for temptations of the flesh may have similarities to the passionate ideologue who seeks expression in terrorism and assured self-destruction. To relate religious or political passions to infantile wishes or drives is not to denigrate them. Although one must be cautious about excessive reductionism in recognizing that this behavior has sources that go beyond drive derivatives and includes aspects of ego function (identifications, ideals, etc.), this view offers a unifying framework for an understanding of the various meanings of passion, so seemingly disparate on the surface.

The Psychoanalytic Literature

The only direct reference to passion in the *Standard Edition* of Freud is in the *Introductory Lectures,* where he speaks about universal dream symbolism and states: "wild animals mean people in an excited sensual state and further evil instincts and passions."[4] Loewald, in his discussion of transference, speaks briefly of individuals who have a passion for the transference, and refers to similar comments by both Freud and Ferenczi. He offers no references.[5] Michels's comments about passion are pertinent, even though they are directed to the student rebels of the late 1960s. He states:

> from a psychological point of view, passion is quite different from patterns of either thought or action because, unlike these, it cannot be compartmentalized or isolated from other personality functions. True passion organizes an individual's life, his every thought and action, and allows no compromise. It is, to borrow a phrase, 'nonnegotiable'."[6]

Benedek, following Landauer, focuses on ambivalence, the fear of death, and merger in the passionate act of love making. She emphasizes idealization of the love object as well as the confirmation of one's worth with attendant elevated self-esteem.[7] Kernberg has offered one of the most extensive discussions of passion in psychoanalytic literature.[8] He discusses many issues including mystery, the longing for the incestuous object, and superego responses, the crossing of self and object boundaries, and pregenital aggression. In particular he distinguishes the view of passion as an early stage of a love relationship from the idea of its being the cement of a more enduring one, and includes elements of the former in the latter:

> Secrets and mystery shared by the couple increase their freedom from the surrounding conventional social world and secrets and mystery of each partner maintain and create new boundaries in the couple's relationship. Secrets and mystery derive from the continuing redefinition of life in the present as new tasks, challenges, and crises reactivate conflicts and needs from the past and bring about subtle changes and actualization of unknown potentials, which may bring the couple closer together or distance them. (p. 111)

THE ATTRIBUTES AND PSYCHODYNAMICS OF PASSION

What are the important attributes of passionate attachment? A passage in *Gantenbein*, a novel by Max Frisch, richly describes a marital relationship that maintains affectionate ties, but has lost the quality of passion. In so doing Frisch masterfully describes aspects of passion. Humorously and imaginatively he plays with multiple scenarios that might have taken place in the lives of his two main male protagonists, Gantenbein and Enderlin. In important measure, the book is about the relationships between men and women:

So there you rest, a couple with bodies dead to love all night long in your joint bedroom . . . you make love. What business is that of other people's? It's refreshing, but it's not worth a confession. . . . Then again the gentle disappearance of all curiosity on both sides, not uttered and scarcely shown; only camouflaged behind the demands of the day. . . . What remains is affection, the quiet and deep and almost unshakable affection. Is that nothing? . . . Nothing will be wilder than your love in the old days, at best it will be just the same. Was it wild? You don't speak about that. In tender protection of the present. . . . How can you bear the fact that you understand each other so well, better and better, so sexlessly, as though you weren't still, seen as bodies, a man and a woman? Then you suddenly seek grounds for jealousy. Without it, God knows, your deadly comradeship would be complete. A stupid incident on the beach, a natural, easy embrace among pine trees, which remain the unforgettable thing about it, an infidelity that happened years ago, cursed in anguish, then of course forgotten, her name or his name is preserved in silence like the Crown Jewels, uttered only in extreme conversations, hence rarely, once or twice a year, so that it shan't get worn out like the love of your bodies. . . . you live in the everyday again, which is truth, with pyjamas and a toothbrush in your foamy mouth in front of the other, with classical nakedness in the bath that does not excite, intimate, you talk in the bathroom about the guests who have just left, and about the intellectual world that links you. You understand each other, without having to agree. Now isn't Now, but Always. . . . you long jointly . . . but not for each other. . . . You talk about a trip in autumn, a trip together, you suddenly long for a country that actually exists, you could go there in autumn. No one will stop you. You don't need a rope ladder in order to kiss, and no hiding place, and there are no nightingales and no lark to warn you it is time to leave, no myrmidons force you together, no prohibition, no fear that your amorous sin will be found out. You are approved of. You don't enquire into your story; that is well known, so to speak. The calendar of your early times has long since been emended; a selection of names and dates and places, at first bold in its incompleteness, than carefully completed, has been closed for years. Why should you now, at two in the morning before a strenuous week-day, explore your past again? Confession with its joys has been used up, trust is complete, curiosity abandoned, the other's early life is a book you think you know as you know a classic, a bit dusty already. . . . The past is no secret any longer, the present is thin because it is worn out day by day, and the future means growing old. . . ." (pp. 127–30)

Elements of this theme are repeated in Ingmar Bergman's *Scenes from a Marriage.* Johan and Marianne have a perfect marriage from which Johan must escape to a relationship with an unsuitable woman. This new passionate relationship creates a dramatic change in the sense of reality: joy and excitement of the new, generated by the search for novelty and its attendant satisfaction, are combined with apprehension and anxiety at the loss of the familiar and stable. No less important is the evocation of the self in a new role, a creative act which allows a new aspect of the personality to emerge, one that incidentally leads to Johan's downfall. It is not without significance that ten years after their rupture Johan and Marianne, each remarried, find passion again in a *clandestine* relationship which they reestablish with one another.

Among the enemies of passion are: absolute understanding and knowledge of the other; familiarity; certainty; predictability and repetition; absolute trust in the other and the disarming of jealousy; and legitimization of the relationship, precluding the sense of transgression.

But what of the relationship of passion to romantic love? Romance is related to chivalry and is defined as a fictitious narrative (in prose) of which the scene and incidents are very remote from those of ordinary life. The elements of invention, story, wanton exaggeration, the imaginary, fabulous, and fictitious characters having no foundation in fact, all figure heavily in the definition provided by the OED. The elements of passion begin to assert themselves as one recognizes the dominant thrust of wishfulness in opposition to reality, logic, and realistic appraisal. Closely allied to wishfulness is a state of feeling, multifaceted, but characterized especially by its intensity, and by the high state of arousal; by virtue of its intensity it becomes the grand organizer of the individual's life. Everything else takes a secondary role. Passion's very intensity and divorce from reality make it an unstable state except in those cases of brittle erotomania which by virtue of their persistent illusory nature and divorce from reality are psychotic. Separations between lovers, as in the classical medieval romance, favor the maintenance of passion, for contact and confrontation support reality and undo illusion.

Beyond illusion, passion has to do with mystery, with the unknown, with elusiveness and even with impenetrability. Something that constantly escapes one's grasp encourages a continued pursuit of the unknown. The mystery itself involves an illusion. And that illusion includes the wonderful things that remain to be discovered. In this respect passionate lovers are mutual teachers, but they are teachers about life and the mystery of life. Paradoxically, in the passionate relationship there is reserve. All is not revealed: there is some degree of uncertainty. A patient speaking of a brief passion of times past spoke of the woman as a courtesan. Without words she communicated strong, exciting signals of availability. "It reminded me of medieval times. Eye beams blew me away. Power flew through the air like a laser beam." Yet beyond the passionate embrace, there was an elusiveness about this woman reflected in her sultriness, in her markedly different life experience. Opposites attract. Though passion is not dissolved by sexual gratification, there is always more to be desired. Possession is incomplete—an aspect of passion to which I will return.

The importance of the issue of mystery was expressed very richly by the wife of the man who organized the underwater search for what remained of the SS *Andrea Doria*. She describes her husband's passionate involvement with this sunken ship and his intense curiosity for what was in the safe that was recovered. I quote loosely:

> When that ship went down, my husband, thirty years ago, dove to look at her. It did something that every woman hopes to do

to a man. It hooked him. He could not forget her and it filled
him with mystery."

When she was asked about the opening of the safe and the
examination of the contents that was to occur the following
day, she said: "if I had my way, that safe would never be
opened. It would remain forever a mystery." Though disappointment greeted the opening of the safe, which was devoid
of anything of value or of interest, the discovery of a boundless
treasure would no less have dissolved the mystery and ended
the passion.

Closely akin to mystery and of special importance to passionate attachment is the element of danger which lies in the forbidden and the secret. The fantasy of transgression with its associated danger increases the excitement and pleasure of a passionate
relationship. As Woody Allen put it, "If sex isn't dirty, you
must be doing something wrong." The unconscious infantile
origins of these fantasies will be discussed later. But even the
conscious component of transgression (the lovers against the
world, Romeo and Juliet in opposition to their *families*), involves
the need to savor moments stolen from the world and the
expectations of the world. These aspects of the experience of
passionate attachments heighten the pleasure.

The intense emotional experience of passionate love includes
components of many feelings and many fantasies, all of which
increase the state of arousal and the sense of pleasure. Not
the least is the feeling of jealousy. The passionate lover is a
jealous lover, one who wishes to possess totally, and for whom
possession is ever incomplete or uncertain, a goal to be constantly sought.

Dangers of other sorts underlie the anxiety which is a component of the passionate state. A patient in analysis ushered in a
discussion of passionate relationships with anticipatory dreams
of being killed by a woman and battling in the Middle Ages
with a group of women. In a final dream he is in a struggle
with a snake which is as thick and pink as a penis, yet as he
tries to strangle it, its mouth opens up and becomes a frightening
vagina. His associations made it apparent that he was struggling
with fears of being devoured by a woman and of merging
with her. At the same time he was excited by the theft of a

woman's underwear. These dreams were followed by the revelation and discussion of a number of passionate relationships.
In this situation the sense of danger and illicit possession accompanied and heightened the experience of passionate love. Unconscious fantasies of a search for forbidden objects underlie
the guilty sense of transgression and heighten the pleasurable
excitement.

One of the most powerful aspects of a new passionate relationship is the formation of a new sense of self. In this discussion
I will avoid the complex theoretical controversy that surrounds
the use of concept, self. What I refer to is a self-representation,
with conscious and unconscious components. This is the tem-
plate of self-perception that guides the person in the real world,
that determines his actions, that effects his perception of others.
It is a product of wishes and experience and, though a structure,
is capable in two respects of modification in the context of
constant commerce with the world. The first is in the domain
of mastery, the developing sense of competence that occurs
as individuals confront the world. This includes the body-representation, which involves a set of presumptions of what one
can expect from one's body, and what one can expect one's
body to do. The other domain is that of relationships with
objects. Self-representations become more defined as the cogni-
tive capacity and emotional resources of the developing infant,
in interaction with the world, permit him to separate himself
from objects. As development occurs, complex and more
nuanced constellations of self and object arise, each object evok-
ing a somewhat different and unique sense of self. In this regard
one can speak of different self and object constellations, each
with qualities that make it somewhat different from others,
but all related to an integrated core that has been loosely called
identity. In experiential terms (object relationships), each person
is a somewhat different person with each other person. A passionate relationship involves the consolidation of a new self-
object constellation.

Ideal self-representations play a part in the formation of the
new self-representations in the context of passionate relationships. These ideal representations in part have their origins in
the frustration of childhood wishes and represent wishes to
achieve what has not been attained in the past; omnipotence,

success in sibling and oedipal rivalries, total possession of the love object, etc. The unconscious illusion of at least partial gratification of these desires in requited passionate love leads to the approximation of aspects of the ego ideal which is associated with a euphoric sense of fullness. At the same time the fantasy of attaining these forbidden wishes is echoed in the excitement of the transgression which may accompany passion. By achieving the ideal self one becomes the person one wishes to be in the catalytic presence of the other.

Unconsciously there resides in all of us, cordoned off from reality, the wish to achieve the sublime. It is this wish in all of its power that is activated as the passionate relationship develops, and passion for a time escapes the constraints of reality as one finds oneself in a passionate embrace.

· · ·

Passionate love is what you want it to be, is what you make it, is what you can allow yourself to experience with and without fear. It is a gratifying and powerful illusion, but to say that is in no way to devalue it, for once it is experienced and reciprocated it is the closest thing to ever-elusive happiness. It is for this reason that when one lists the external attributes of the loved object, such as the beauty of the person, his or her intelligence, wit, sparkle, directness, freedom, the object's presumed appearance to others of importance in one's life—one touches on elements but one does not encapsulate the whole. True, but insufficient as explanations in a similar way, are the issues of idealization of the loved object, and the sense of being the ideal object in the eyes of the lover. It does come closer to the core, however, to say that one can be oneself in the lover's presence and to like it, to be closer to what one ideally would become. And here the catalyzing issue becomes important. We are each of us many people for better or worse. What is it about the loved person that permits the lover to reveal and to become the person that he would like to be, the sexual person, the generous person, the giving person, the strong person, the person capable of tolerating pain, the passionate person—in short the worthy person, the person who truly deserves the love of his lover? Here one must distinguish clearly between deserving and being entitled. Love immediately dissolves when one feels entitled to another's love. Also, one does not earn the love of another person. One has the love of another person because one is, and thereupon it follows naturally.

The issue of lovers mutually catalyzing the development of new images of the other is of special importance in the passionate relationship. It begins with very small and incremental interactions. Here with some trepidation I paraphrase Frisch. Gantenbein sees a woman, Lila. She has the physical attributes of beauty. She begins to talk. Instantaneously her appearance changes. She becomes more beautiful by the words she utters. Lust, lying dormant, ever ready to emerge, begins to consolidate the picture. Intensity has developed but passion has not yet emerged. Gantenbein and Lila are now in a new and uncertain phase. Possibilities exist but there is a long path to negotiate. Lila leaves on a trip to perform in a play, for she is an actress, or perhaps to give a lecture, for she may be a university professor—no matter. What could be a more nurturant climate for the development of passionate love than the wonderful power of Gantenbein's imaginative fantasy? What better preparation for the renewed encounter than the richness of possibilities explored by Gantenbein in his imaginings of how he will be with his lover and as a lover! Thought and fantasy merge as trial action *without* necessary cost or danger. And then the re-encounter, a re-encounter fortified by all of the possibilities of what he would want to be for Lila and what he would like her to be for him. What joy in this re-encounter as Gantenbein realizes this ideal in action, in being—no longer in fantasy, but in being. And then there is the reciprocation, the confirmation, hopefully, of the fantasy of what Lila is like. And so on. Or consider the alternative: sadly and painfully, Gantenbein meets Lila. She talks frivolously and insensitively of an experience she has had. Disappointment. The illusion is lost.

The paths toward the individual experience of passionate love may diverge. The lovers in a passionate encounter may not experience absolutely reciprocal feelings and behaviors. The patient mentioned previously brings this issue to the fore. Although passionately in love he continued to work effectively at a demanding university—inspired and invigorated by his current state. But his lover's passion left her unable to work under these circumstances. Clearly the partners experienced their passion in different ways. He was exalted and energized by the sense of loving and being loved. She was so absorbed in the relationship that she could not attend to the world. In each the passion was powerful in its own way.

But what is it that sets passion in motion and permits it to develop? The circumstances that antecede the development of passionate love vary throughout the life cycle. It is traditional to view passion as the prerogative of the young, given as they are to greater fluidity of self-definition, pressured to explore new roles, and inclined to greater reactivity to the inevitable and sharp disappointments in life, as yet unmuted by the experience of time. Clearly flux and instability may lead to a search for passion.

Yet the very conditions of stability and defined accomplishment may be the impetus for a search for passion in middle age. One might consider middle age from the point of view of its special characteristics in relationship to stability and change. The experience of the rapid flight of time that characterizes childhood and early adulthood is in part reflective of the kaleidoscope of rapid environmental change. As adulthood proceeds there is a general movement toward greater stability and decreased rapidity of change in work, love, friendships, etc. What has been described as "burn-out" is at least in part a reflection of this external stability and is associated with relentless and leaden repetition of experience. One must view this stability therefore from the point of view both of its positive and negative aspects. On the positive side is the defined sense of self that has been generated by the solid accretions which stem from repeated successes and mastery in one's life. Thus fortified the middle-aged individual may be well prepared to deal with situations and wishes that have been long unattended. The richness of experience which includes both success and failure crystalizes a self-perception in the adult as a person who can be depended upon for better or worse in commerce with the world. A defined self-perception fortifies one for a confrontation with the new. It is easy to see how the search for change, the search for the new, the search for mystery can lead to a passionate experience that will act as a powerful antidote to frustration, disappointment, and repetition. So it is that at certain moments of chronic or acute crisis individuals become available for and seek out passionate love. In seeking the new, they unconsciously search for gratification of the old—the attainment of unachieved and forbidden childhood wishes. And this is part of the mystery.

Passionate love in healthy form is not enduring and under the best of circumstances gives way to its more muted counterpart, affectionate love. Since passionate love is so dominated by fantasy, it is best insulated from reality. Hence the passionate love of the medieval romance could flourish and be nurtured by continued separations, non-consummation of sexual love, and the elaboration of all-consuming fantasy unencumbered by the reality of encounter. Distance and non-consummation therefore are a fertile soil for long lasting passionate love. Erotomania, the pathological counterpart of passionate love, persists by virtue of its characteristic disregard of reality.

Though inevitably the intensity of passion must diminish, it has varied future courses—it may be gradually muted to become a powerful affectionate relationship which is substantial and persistent, or it may dissolve as with the dissolution of an illusion. In either case there is much that remains, for the new self-object constellation—conceived apart from reality and partially indifferent to it, sustained by wishful fantasies of childhood—has a transforming power and leaves a residue. The self-representation created in the new experience is a new representation, not entirely divorced from the old, but with elements of hope and potentiality that enrich it, make it fuller and permit a wider range of possibilities for future relationships.

One of the problems in understanding passionate love is that it is an entirely personal and subjective experience. In this, appropriately, it resembles pain. When one experiences passion one is never sure of how much it approximates the experience of the partner. In this respect, it is probably one of the most complex of emotional states, not only by virtue of its being compounded by many other emotions but also by the myriad of memories, fantasies, and wishes, all part of one's own unique life experience and always acting on both conscious as well as unconscious levels. It would seem, therefore, that the trouble we have in defining it is that it has no absolute general definition. For this reason I have underlined some of the attributes of passionate love—change in reality, transgression, illusion; the imagining and the formation of a new self under the catalytic influence of the other; impenetrability, and above all mystery, a mystery that makes passion elusive for those who wish to understand it, and especially for those who wish to experience it.

Passionate Attachments in the West in Historical Perspective

LAWRENCE STONE

Central to the argument of this chapter is a proposition put forward by my colleague Robert Darnton:

> One thing seems clear to everyone who returns from field work: other people are other. They do not think the way we do. And if we want to understand their way of thinking, we should set out with the idea of capturing otherness.[1]

What this means is that we cannot assume that people in the past—even in our own Western Judeo-Christian world—thought about and felt passionate attachments the way we do.

My remarks will be confined to the two most common of passionate attachments—between two adolescents or adults of different sexes, and between mothers and children. I know there are other attachments—between homosexuals, siblings, fathers and children—but they are not of such central importance as the first two. Before we can begin to examine the very complex issue of passionate attachments in the past, we therefore have to make a fundamental distinction between attachment between two sexually mature persons, usually of the opposite gender, and attachment to the child of one's body.

In the former case, the problem is how to distinguish what is generally known as falling in love from two other human conditions. The first of those conditions is an urgent desire for sexual intercourse with a particular individual, a passion for sexual access to the body of the person desired. In this particular instance the libido is for some reason closely focussed upon a specific body, rather than there being a general state of sexual excitement capable of satisfaction by any promiscuous coupling. The second condition is one of settled and well-tried ties which develop between two people who have known each other for a long time and have come to trust each other's judgment and have confidence in each other's loyalty and affection. This condition of caring may or may not be accompanied by exciting sexual bonding, and may or may not have begun with falling in love, a phase of violent and irrational psychological passion, which does not last very long.

Historians and anthropologists are in general agreement that romantic love—this usually brief but very intensely felt and all-consuming attraction towards another person—is culturally conditioned, and therefore common only in certain societies at certain times, or even in certain social groups within those societies—usually the elite, with the leisure to cultivate such feelings. They are, however, less certain whether or not romantic love is merely a culture-induced sublimated psychological overlay on top of the biological drive for sex, or whether it has biochemical roots which operate quite independently from the libido. Would anyone in fact "fall in love" if they had not read about it or heard it talked about? Did poetry invent love, or love poetry?

Some things can be said with certainty about the history of the phenomenon. The first is that cases of romantic love can be found at all times and places and have often been the subject of powerful poetic expression, from the Song of Solomon to Shakespeare. On the other hand, neither social approbation nor the actual experience of romantic love is at all common to all societies, as anthropologists have discovered. Second, historical evidence for romantic love before the age of printing is largely confined to elite groups, which of course does not mean that it may not have occurred lower down the social scale among illiterates. As a socially approved cultural artifact it began in Europe in the southern French aristocratic courts in the twelfth century, made fashionable by a group of poets, the troubadours. In this case the culture dictated that it should occur between an unmarried male and a married woman, and that it should either go sexually unconsummated or should be adulterous. This cultural ideal certainly spread into wider circles in the middle ages—witness the love story of Aucassin and Nicolette—but it should be noted that none of these models end happily.

By the sixteenth and seventeenth centuries, our evidence for the first time becomes quite extensive, thanks to the spread of literacy and the printing press. We now have love poems, like Shakespeare's Sonnets, love letters, and autobiographies by women primarily concerned with their love life. All the courts of Europe were evidently hotbeds of passionate intrigues and liaisons, some romantic, some sexual. The printing press began to spread pornography to a wider public, thus stimulating the libido, while the plays of Shakespeare indicate that romantic love was a familiar concept to society at large, who composed his audience.

Whether this romantic love was approved of, however, is another question. We simply do not know how Shakespearean audiences reacted to Romeo and Juliet. Did they, like us, and as Shakespeare clearly intended, fully identify with the young lovers? Or, when they left the theatre, did they continue to act like the Montague and Capulet parents, who were trying to stop these irresponsible adolescents from allowing an ephemeral and irrational passion to interfere with the serious business of politics and patronage? What is certain is that every advice book, every medical treatise, every sermon and religious homily of the sixteenth and seventeenth centuries firmly rejected both romantic passion and lust as suitable bases for marriage.[2] In the sixteenth century marriage was thought to be best arranged by parents, who could be relied upon to choose socially and economically suitable partners who would enhance the prestige and importance of the kin group as a whole. It was believed that the sexual bond would automatically create the necessary harmony between the two strangers in order to maintain the stability of the new family unit. This, it seems, is not an unreasonable assumption, since recent investigations in Japan have shown that there is no difference in the rate of divorce between couples whose marriages were arranged by their parents and couples whose marriages were made by individual choice based on romantic love. The arranged and the romantic marriage each has an equal chance of turning out well, or breaking up.[3]

Public admiration for marriage-for-love is thus a fairly recent occurrence in Western society, arising out of the romantic movement of the late eighteenth century, and only winning general acceptance in the twentieth. In the eighteenth century orthodox opinion about marriage shifted away from subordinating the individual will to the interests of the group, and away from economic or political considerations towards those of well-tried personal affection. The ideal marriage of the eighteenth century was one preceded by three to six months of intensive courting, between a couple from families roughly equal in social status and economic wealth, a courtship which only took place with the prior consent of parents on both sides. A sudden falling head over heels in love, although a familiar enough psychological phenomenon, was thought of as a mild form of insanity, in which judgment and prudence are cast aside, all the inevitable imperfections of the loved one become invisible, and wholly unrealistic dreams of everlasting happiness possess the mind of the afflicted victim. Fortunately, in most cases the disease is of short duration, and the patient normally makes a full recovery. To the eighteenth century, the main object of society—church, law, government, and parents—was to prevent the victim from taking some irrevocable step, particularly from getting married. This is why most European countries made marriage under the age of 21 or even later illegal and invalid unless carried out with the consent of parents or guardians. In England this became law in 1753. Runaway marriages based on passionate attachments still took place, but they were made as difficult as possible to carry out, and in most countries were virtually impossible.

It was not, therefore, until the romantic movement and the

rise of the novel, especially the pulp novel, in the nineteenth century, that society at large accepted a new idea—that it was normal and indeed praiseworthy for young men and women to fall passionately in love, and that there must be something wrong with those who have failed to have such an overwhelming experience some time in late adolescence or early manhood. Once this new idea was publicly accepted, the dictation of marriage by parents came to be regarded as intolerable and immoral.

Today, the role of passionate attachments between adults in our society is obscured by a new development, the saturation of the whole culture—through every medium of communication—with sexuality as the predominant and overriding human drive, a doctrine whose theoretical foundations were provided by Freud. In no past society known to me has sex been given so prominent a role in the culture at large, nor has sexual fulfillment been elevated to such preeminence in the list of human aspirations—in a vain attempt to relieve civilization of its discontents. If Thomas Jefferson today was asked to rewrite the Declaration of Independence he would certainly have to add total sexual fulfillment to "Life, Liberty and Human Happiness" as one of the basic natural rights of every member of society. The traditional restraints upon sexual freedom—religious and social taboos, and the fear of pregnancy and venereal disease—have now been almost entirely removed. We find it scarcely credible today that in most of Western Europe in the seventeenth century, in a society whose marriage age was postponed into the late twenties, a degree of chastity was practiced that kept the illegitimacy rate—without contraceptives—as low as 2 or 3 percent. Only in Southern Ireland does such a situation still exist—according to one hypothesis, due to a lowering of the libido caused by large-scale consumption of Guinness Stout. Under these conditions, it seems to me almost impossible today to distinguish passionate attachment in the psychological sense—meaning love—from passionate attachment in the physical sense—meaning lust. But the enormous success today of pulp fiction concerned almost exclusively with romantic rather than physical love shows that women at least still hanker after the experience of falling in love. Whether the same applies to men is more doubtful, so that there may be a real gender gap on this subject today, which justifies this distinction I am making between love and lust.

To sum up, the historian can see a clear historical trend in the spread of the cultural concept of romantic love in the West, beginning in court circles in the twelfth century, and expanding outward from the sixteenth century on. It received an enormous boost with the rise of the romantic novel, and another boost with the achievement of near-total literacy by the end of the nineteenth century. Today, however, it is so intertwined with sexuality, that it is almost impossible to distinguish between the two. Both, however, remain clearly distinct from caring, that is well-tried and settled affection based on long-term commitment and familiarity.

It is also possible to say something about the changing relationship of passionate love to marriage. For all classes who possessed property, that is the top two-thirds economically, marriage before the seventeenth century was arranged by the parents, and the motives were the economic and political benefit of the kin group, not the emotional satisfaction of the individuals. As the concept of individualism grew in the seventeenth and eighteenth centuries, it slowly became accepted that the prime object was "holy matrimony," a sanctified state of monogamous married contentment. This was best achieved by allowing the couple to make their own choice, provided that both sets of parents agreed that the social and economic gap was not too wide, and that marriage was preceded by a long period of courtship. By the eighteenth and nineteenth centuries, individualism had so far taken precedence over the group interests of the kin that the couple were left more or less free to make their own decision, except in the highest aristocratic and royal circles. Today individualism is given such absolute priority in most Western societies, that the couple are virtually free to act as they please, to sleep with whom they please, and to marry and divorce when and whom they please to suit their own pleasure. The psychic cost of such behavior, and its self-defeating consequences, are becoming clear, however, and how long this situation will last is anybody's guess.

Here I should point out that the present-day family—I exclude the poor black family in America from this generalization—is not, as is generally supposed, disintegrating because of a very high divorce rate of up to 50 percent. It has to be remembered that the median duration of marriage today is almost exactly the same as it was 100 years ago. Divorce, in short, now acts as a functional substitute for death: both are means of terminating marriage at a premature stage. It may well be that the psychological effects on the survivor may be very different, although in most cases the catastrophic economic consequences for the woman remain the same. But the point to be emphasized is that broken marriages, stepchildren, and single-parent households were as common in the past as they are today, the only difference being the mechanism which has brought about this situation.

The most difficult historical problem concerns the role of romantic love among the propertyless poor, who comprised about one-third of the population. Since they were propertyless, their loves and marriages were of little concern to their kin, and they were therefore more or less free to choose their own mates. By the eighteenth century, and probably before, court records make it clear that these groups often married for love, combined with a confused set of motives including lust and the economic necessity to have a strong and healthy assistant to run the farm or the shop. It was generally expected that they would behave "lovingly" towards each other, but this often did not happen. In many a peasant marriage, the husband seems to have valued his cow more than his wife. Passionate attachments among the poor certainly occurred, but how often they took priority over material interests we may never know for certain.[4]

All that we do know is that courting among the poor normally lasted six months or more, and that it often involved all-night sessions alone together in the dark in a room with a bed, usually with the knowledge and consent of the parents or masters. Only relatively rarely, and only at a late stage after engagement, did full sexual intercourse commonly take place during these nights, but it is certain that affectionate conversation, and discussion of the possibilities of marriage, were accompanied by embracing and kissing, and probably also by what today is euphemistically called "heavy petting." This practice of "bundling," as it was called, occurred in what was by our standards an extremely prudish, and indeed sexually innocent, society. When men and women went to bed together they almost invariably kept on a piece of clothing, a smock or a shirt, to conceal their nakedness. Moreover the sexual act itself was almost always carried out in the "missionary" position. The evidence offered in the courts in cases of divorce in the pre-modern period provide little evidence of that polymorphous perversity advocated in the sex manuals available in every bookstore today.

What is certain is that even after this process of intimate physical and verbal courtship had taken place, economic factors still loomed large in the final decision by both parties about whether or not to marry. Thus passion and material interest were in the end inextricably involved, but it is important to stress that, among the poor, material interest only became central at the *end* of the process of courtship instead of at the beginning, as was the case with the rich.

If an early modern peasant said "I love a woman with ten acres of land," just what did he mean? Did he lust after the body of the woman? Did he admire her good health, administrative and intellectual talents and strength of character as a potential housekeeper, income producer, and mother of his children? Was he romantically head over heels in love with her? Or did he above all prize her for her ten acres? Deconstruct the text as we wish, there is no way of getting a clear answer to that question; and in any case, if we could put that peasant on the couch today and interrogate him, it would probably turn out that he merely felt that he liked the woman more because of her ten acres.

Finally, we know that in the eighteenth century at least half of all brides in England and America were pregnant on their wedding day. But this tells us more about sexual customs than about passionate attachments: sex began at the moment of engagement, and marriage in church came later, often triggered by the pregnancy. We also know that if a poor servant girl was impregnated by her master, which often happened, the latter usually had no trouble finding a poor man who would marry her, in return for payment of ten pounds or so. Not much passionate attachment there, among any of the three persons involved.

· · ·

The second type of passionate attachment is that which develops between the parent, especially the mother, and the child. Here again as historians we are faced with the intractable problem of nature versus nurture, of the respective roles of biology and culture. The survival of the species demands that the female adult should take optimum care of the child over a long period, to ensure its survival. This is particularly necessary among humans since the child is born prematurely compared with all other primates, because of its exaggerated cranial size, and so is peculiarly helpless for an exceptionally long period of time. Moreover, experiments with primates have shown that it is close body contact in the first weeks of life which creates the strong bond between mother and child. A passionate attachment of the mother for its child therefore seems to be both a biological necessity for survival and an emotional reality.

On the other hand recorded human behavior indicates that cultural traditions and economic necessity often override this biological drive. For over 90 percent of human history man has been a hunter-gatherer, and it is impossible for a woman to carry two babies and perform her daily task of gathering. Barring sexual abstention, which seems unlikely, some form of infanticide must therefore have been a necessity, dictated by economic conditions.

Other factors came into play in more recent times. From at least classical antiquity to the eighteenth century it was normal in northwest Europe to swaddle all babies at birth—that is to tie them up head to foot in bandages, taken off only to remove the urine and feces. This automatically reduced body contact with the mother, and therefore presumably the bonding effect between mother and child. Secondly, all women who could afford to do so put their infants out to wet-nurse from birth to about the age of two. The prime reason for this among the more well-to-do was undoubtedly the accepted belief that sexual excitement spoils the milk. Few husbands were willing to do without the sexual services of their wives for that length of time, hence the reliance on a wet nurse. But this meant that for all except the tiny minority who could afford to take the nurse into the house, the child was removed within a few days of birth and put in the care of a village woman some distance from the home. Under these conditions affection between parents and children could not begin to grow until the child returned to the home at about the age of eighteen months or two years, and the child might well have a more passionate relationship with its nurse than with its mother—as was the case with Shakespeare's Juliet.

In any case, the child's return to its mother would only take place if it did not die while with the wet nurse. There is overwhelming evidence that the mortality rate of children being wet-nursed was very much higher than that of children being breast-fed by their mothers, and contemporaries were well aware of this. It is difficult to avoid the suspicion that one incentive for the practice, particularly for its enormous expansion in France in the nineteenth century, was as an indirect method of infanticide, out of sight and out of mind. This suspicion is reinforced by the huge numbers of children in the eighteenth and nineteenth centuries who were abandoned and deposited in workhouses or foundling hospitals, only a small fraction of whom survived the experience. Whatever the intention, in practice the foundling hospitals of London or Paris acted as a socially acceptable means of family limitation after birth. Few women other than those who gave birth to bastard children practiced infanticide themselves, if only because the risks were too great. But overlaying and stifling by accident while in the same bed during the night, putting out to wet-nurse, abandoning to public authorities, or depositing in foundling hospitals served the same purpose. Unwanted children of the poor and not so poor were somehow or other got rid of in all these socially acceptable ways.[5]

These common eighteenth and even nineteenth century practices, especially prevalent in France, raise questions about the degree of maternal love in that society. This is not an easy question to answer, and historians are deeply divided on this issue. Some point to evidence of mothers who were devoted to their children and seriously disturbed by their premature deaths. Others point to the bleak statistics of infant mortality: about 25 percent dead before the age of two, a percentage deliberately increased by wet-nursing, abandonment, and infanticide by neglect—practices which have been described as "post-natal family planning." A mid–nineteenth century Bavarian woman summed up the emotional causes and consequences:

The parents are glad to see the first and second child, especially if there is a boy amongst them. But all that come after aren't so heartily welcome. Anyway not many of these children live. Four out of a dozen at most, I suppose. The others very soon get to heaven. When little children die, it's not often that you have a lot of grief. They're little angels in heaven.[6]

Another question is how kindly children were treated if they did survive. I have suggested that sixteenth and early seventeenth century societies were cold and harsh, relatively indifferent to children, and resorting to frequent and brutal whippings from an early age as the only reliable method of discipline. Calvinism, with its grim insistence on original sin, encouraged parents and schoolmasters to whip children, in order quite literally to beat the Hell out of them. I have argued that only in the eighteenth century did there develop a more optimistic view of the infant as a plain sheet of paper upon which good or evil could be written by the process of cultural socialization. The more extreme view of Rousseau, that the child is born good, in a state of innocence, was widely read, but not very widely accepted, so far as can be seen—for the rather obvious reason that it is contradicted by the direct experience of all observant parents.

To sum up, first there is ample evidence for the widespread practice of infanticide in societies ignorant of contraception, a practice which, disguised in socially acceptable forms, lasted well into the nineteenth century. Second, children, even of the rich, were often treated with calculated brutality in the sixteenth and seventeenth centuries, and again in the nineteenth, in order to eradicate original sin; the eighteenth and twentieth centuries are two rare periods of educational permissiveness. As for the poor, they have always regarded children very largely as potential economic assets and treated them accordingly. Their prime functions have been to help in the house, the workshop, and the field, to add to the family income, and to support their parents in old age. How much room was left over from these economic considerations for passionate attachment, even with the mother, remains an open question.

· · ·

Passionate attachments between young people can and do happen in any society as a byproduct of biological sexual attraction, but the social acceptability of the emotion has varied enormously over time and class and space, determined primarily by cultural norms and property arrangements. Furthermore, though there is a strong biological component in the passionate attachment of mothers to children, it too is often overlaid by economic necessities, by religious views about the nature of the child, and by accepted cultural practices such as wet-nursing. We are in a unique position today in that society, through social security and other devices, has taken over the economic responsibilities of children for their aged parents; contraception is normal and efficient; our culture is dominated by romantic notions of passionate love as the only socially admissible reason for marriage; and sexual fulfillment is accepted as the dominant human drive and a natural right for both sexes. Behind all this there lies a frenetic individualism, a restless search for the sexual and emotional ideal in human relationships, and a demand for instant ego gratification which is inevitably self-defeating and ultimately destructive.

Most of this is new and unique to our culture. It is, therefore, quite impossible to extrapolate from present values and behavior to those in the past. Historical others—even our own forefathers and mothers—were indeed other.

Four Mischievous
Theories of Sex:
Demonic, Divine, Casual,
and Nuisance

WILLIAM F. MAY

Several conflicting attitudes toward sex beset us today. We loosely associate these attitudes with the behavior of different cultural groups. Whether the groups actually behaved in these ways poses a descriptive question that will not preoccupy me for the moment. I am interested more in the attitudes than in the historical accuracy of the symbols. The Victorian prude feared sex as demonic; romantics, such as D. H. Lawrence, elevated sex to the divine; liberals tend to reduce sex to the casual; and the British, as the satirists relentlessly portray them, pass it off as a nuisance. I will argue that all these views of sex contain an element of truth; all are ultimately mischievous; and most can be found conflicting and concurrent in ourselves.

Sex as Demonic

Those who fear sex as the demon in the groin reckon with sex as a power which, once let loose, tends to grip and destroy its host; it is self-destructive and destructive of others, a loose cannon, as it were, in human affairs. Our movies and drugstore paperbacks relentlessly mock this view, which we tend to assign remotely to our Victorian forebears and proximately to our parents. While parents, in fact, may fear the explosive power of sex in their adolescent children, it is doubtful whether most parents are quite the Victorians their children assume them to be. Children impute this view to their elders because at some level of their being they partly hold to this attitude themselves.

In any event, this pessimism that emphasizes the runaway destructiveness of sex hardly originated with the Victorians. Religiously, it dates back to the Manichaean dualists of the Third Century of the Common Era. Manichaeans divided all reality and power into two rival kingdoms: the Kingdom of God pitted against the Kingdom of Satan, Good versus Evil, Light versus Darkness. They associated the Absolute Good with Spirit and Absolute Evil with Matter. Originally Spirit and Matter existed in an uneasy separation from one another; but through the aggressive strategies of Satan, the present world and humankind came into existence, a sad commingling of them both—Spirit and Flesh. The world is a kind of battleground between these two rival kingdoms. Man's only hope rests in disengaging himself from the pain and confusion and muck of life in the flesh, and allying himself with the Kingdom of Spirit. I say "man" deliberately because the Manichaeans tended to associate women with the intentions of the Devil; that is, with his strategy to perpetuate this present age of confusion and commingling through the device of sex and offspring. Quite literally, marriage in their view is an invention of the Devil, a scheme for perpetuating the human race and the messy world that we know. Man should achieve a final state of metaphysical *Apartheid,* a clean separation from the toils of the flesh, women, and all their issue.

Manichaean sex counselors thus urged on their followers a rigorous ethic of sexual denial—with, however, an antinomian escape clause since not everyone could lead the wholly ascetic life. If one couldn't totally abstain—here is the twist—the Manichaeans believed it was better to engage in "unnatural sex" so as to avoid the risk of progeny. In the Manichaean vision of things, sex is bad, but children are worse. Reproduction should be avoided at all costs since it only perpetuates the grim, woe-beset world that we know. (The mythology sounds strange to the modern ear, but the Manichaeans have served as a symbol of pessimism in later Western theology, and rightly so. A reluctance to have children usually blurts out the pessimism—whatever its causes—of those who think little of the world's present and future prospects.)

Christianity rejected this Manichaean pessimism, and thereby confirmed the religious vision it derived largely from the Scriptures of Israel and from the New Testament. Its monotheism differs from a dualism that takes evil too seriously and that identifies evil too readily with the flesh. Its scriptures highly esteem sexual love (the erotic Song of Solomon would jar in a Manichaean scripture); it grants a sacramental status to marriage; and it describes the body as the temple of the Lord. The lowly, needy, hungering, flatulent body is nothing less than the real estate where the resurrection will occur.

But dualism kept reappearing in the Western tradition, often nesting in Christianity itself or appearing in an alluring alternative, the cult of romantic love. On the surface, the ideal of romantic love, Denis de Rougemont once shrewdly argued, appears to be sexually vigorous; it celebrates God's good green gift of sex. But, in fact, it secretly despairs of sex; it always directs itself to the faraway princess—not to the partner you've got, but to the dream person, the remote figure not yet yours. Sex slips its focus on actual contacts between people and transposes to the realm of the imagination. To possess her is to lose one's appetite for her. Love, therefore, feeds best on obstacles. "We love each other, but you're a Capulet and I'm a Montague." And so it goes from Romeo and Juliet, backward to the Tristan and Iseult myth, and forward to Noel Coward's "Brief Encounter" and the mawkish "Love Story." The poignancy of passion depends upon separation, ultimately upon death. The cult of romantic love locates passion in the teased imagination. The flesh kills; the spirit alone endures; thus Manichaean pessimism hides in its alluring garb.

The post-Renaissance world offered a somewhat drabber

version of this dualist suspicion of sex. Social diseases assaulted the Western countries and associated sex with forces that abuse the mind and body. Further, a concept of marriage emerged with middle-class careerism that encourages a Manichaean wariness toward sex. The bourgeois family depended for its stability and life on the career and the property of the male provider. Premarital sex, which distracts a man from his career and leads him prematurely into marriage, severely limits his prospects. Extramarital sex spoils the marriage itself and public reputation. And marital sex leads to too many children with a cramping effect on the careers of those already arrived. Thus, all told, sex severely inconveniences a careerist-oriented society that depends throughout on deferred gratification.

But not surprisingly, bourgeois culture produced not only repression, but also a pornographic fascination with sex. Sex became, at one and the same time, unmentionable in polite society but also an unshakable obsession in fantasy. Geoffrey Gorer, the English social anthropologist, in his often plagiarized article, "The Pornography of Death," nicely defined all such pornographic preoccupation with sex as an obsession with the sex act abstracted from its natural human emotion, which is *affection*. This definition helps explain the inevitable structure of pornographic novels and films. Invariably, they must proliferate and escalate the varieties of sexual performance. When the sex act separates from its natural human emotion of affection, it loses its tie with the concrete lives of the two persons performing the act; it becomes *boring*. Inevitably, one must reinvest one's interest in the variety of ways and techniques with which the act is performed—one on one, then two on one, then in all possible permutations and combinations, culminating in the orgy. When affection isn't there, it won't do to have bodies perform the act in the age-old ways. Sad variety alone compensates.

(The oft-cited pornographic preoccupation with death and violence today follows the same pattern of escalation. A pornography of death entails an obsession with death and violence abstracted from its natural human emotion, which is grief. Once again such violence, abstracted from persons, inevitably bores, and therefore one must reinvest interest in the technology with which the act is performed. It won't do for James Bond to drive an ordinary General Motors car (as though it weren't death-dealing an instrument enough); he must have a specially equipped vehicle that jets flames out its exhaust. Spies must be killed in all sorts of combinations and permutations. Violence inevitably escalates.)

This ambivalent attitude toward sex that generates both repression and obsession is basically religious—not Jewish or Christian, to be sure, but religious, specifically Manichaean—in its root. It religiously preoccupies itself with sex as a major evil in human affairs.

SEX AS DIVINE

The second of the four attitudes toward sex also qualifies as religious; in this case, however, one elevates sex from the demonic to the divine. D. H. Lawrence offers the definitive expression of this sex-mysticism; let his views stand for the type. *Lady Chatterley's Lover* is a religious book. That assessment didn't occur to people of my generation who, before laying hands on the book, assumed its title was *Lady Chatterley's Lovers,* and settled down for the inevitable orgy. The book offered, however, religion in a very traditional sense, for religion consists of some sort of experience of sacred power perceived in contest with other powers. The sacred grips the subject as overwhelming, alluring, and mysterious, and eventually orders the rest of life for the person or community so possessed. (Exodus 3, for example, describes the contest between Yahveh, God of the Jews, and the power of the Pharaoh. God liberates his people from Egypt and orders their life at Mt. Sinai; God prevails.)

Just so, the novel focuses on a woman who experiences in her own being a contest of the powers—those opposingly symbolized by Lord Clifford, her husband, and Oliver Mellors, her husband's gamekeeper. Her husband possessed those several powers which the English highly prized—status, money, and talent. He was at once an aristocrat, an industrial captain, and an author—an ironmonger and wordmonger. He wielded economic power and word power. Leaving such a man for his gamekeeper would utterly confound the commitments of Lady

Chatterley's class. Lord Clifford's only trouble, his fatal trouble, however, was a war wound that left him dead from the waist down, a state of affairs which was but the natural issue of the kind of destructive power which he wields. Lady Chatterley discovers in the gamekeeper and in the grove where he breeds pheasants, a different kind of power, a growing power in the pheasant and the phallus, and this power prevails.

Lawrence's novel celebrates not random sex but a sex-mysticism. The grove where Lady Chatterley and Oliver meet serves as a sacred precinct removed from the grimy, profane, sooty, industrial midlands of England where men like Lord Clifford ruled. Lawrence explicitly uses the coronation Psalms of Israel to describe the act of sexual intercourse. "Open up, ye everlasting gates, and let the king of glory enter in." In using royal language, Lawrence advocated not sexual promiscuity, as the hungering undergraduates of my generation supposed. Far from it! Lawrence disdained the merely casual affair: he exalted sexual union into a sacred encounter. Tenderhearted sex is the closest we come to salvation in this life. It provides contact with all that nurtures and fulfills. Americans in the 1950s relied on a sentimental marital version of this religious expectation. As the song of the times put it, "love and marriage go together like a horse and carriage." In the oft-called "age of conformity" one tended to look to the sanctuary of marriage to provide respite from the loneliness and pressures of the outer world to which one conformed but which one found unfulfilling.

Sex as Casual

W. H. Auden once observed that the modern liberal offended Lawrence more than the Puritan. The Puritan mistakenly viewed sex as an outsize evil, but the liberal made the even greater mistake of reducing sex to the casual—to one of the many incidental goods which in our liberty we take for granted. Some have called this the drink-of-water theory of sex.

This casual attitude toward sex reflects a liberal industrial culture that prizes autonomy above all else, that reduces nature to raw material to be manipulated and transformed into products of man's own choosing, and that correspondingly reduces the body to the incidental—not to the prison house of the dualists, or to the Lord's temple of the monotheists, or to the sacred grove of the mystics, but to a playground pure and simple.

Some observers argue that this third attitude toward sexual experience dominates our time. Is not D. H. Lawrence, despite his flamboyance, actually somewhat quaint and old-fashioned, the reverse side, if you will, of the Victorian prude? Don't both the prude and the romantic make the mistake of taking sex too seriously? One elevates sex into the satanic, and the other celebrates it as divine. Have we not succeeded in desacralyzing sex and reducing it now to the casual?

This third and apparently prevailing theory of sex today, the so-called new sex ethic, takes two forms. First and most notoriously, its earlier, male chauvinist version converts sex into an instrument of domination. It reduces sex to the casual, by converting women into bunnies and by replacing heterosexuality with a not so latent male orientation. In its magazine formula, it condemns women, flatters the young male, and lavishes on him advice on how to dress, talk, choose his cars, and handle his women—all without involvement. The women's movement has shown proper contempt for this view.

The second version of the new sex ethic avoids the more obvious criticisms of the woman's movement; indeed, it seeks to join it by offering easy access, easy departure, and no long term ties, but with equal rights for both partners. One of our entertainers best summarized this casual, tentative, experimental attitude toward sex and marriage by referring to his decision to do the "marriage bit"—a phrase from show biz. It suggests that marriage offers a role one chooses to play rather than a relationship by which one is permanently altered—not necessarily a one-night stand, but then not likely, either, to run as long as "Life With Father."

This reading of the social history of our time—from the religious to the secular—only apparently persuades. We are not quite as casual about sex as this analysis would suggest. Our popular magazines—men's and women's—may have evangelized for a cool attitude toward sex; but they would not have sold millions of copies if, underneath it all, in the steamy depths of our desires, we could toy with it that easily.

Denis de Rougemont neatly skewers our irrepressible fascination with sex in *The Devil's Share,* a book that included chapters on such topics as the "Devil and Betrayal," the "Devil and War," and the "Devil and Lying." His first sentence in his essay on the "Devil and Sex" reads, in effect: "To the adolescent amongst my readers who have turned to this chapter first . . ." I read de Rougemont's book when I was 32, but the age makes little difference. There one is—young or old—caught red-handed, eyes riveted, imagination stirred, ready for fresh rivulets of knowledge on that most fascinating of topics. Casual curiosity? Yes. But the lure of mystery as well. Elements of the religious as well as the casual characterize our attitude toward the subject.

Sex as a Nuisance

So far, this essay has covered three views of sex; symmetry alone would demand a fourth to complete two sets of paired attitudes. Dualists inflate sex into a transcendent evil; mystics view it as a transcendent good; and casualists reduce it to a trivial good. The demands of symmetry, then, would posit the existence of a fourth group composed of those prosaic folk who dismiss sex as a minor evil, a nuisance. Comic writers have rounded up this particular population and located them in Great Britain under the marquee: "No Sex, Please. We're British." Copulation is, at best, a burdensome ritual to be endured for the sake of a few lackluster goods. One has visions therewith of an underblooded, overarticulate clutch of aristocrats in whom the life force runs thin.

But a report in one of the most popular of American syndicated newspaper columns (in the *Washington Post,* June 14 and 15, 1985) suggests that the number of people occupying the quadrant of petty pessimists may be surprisingly large. Ann Landers asked her reading audience to send a postcard or letter with a reply to the question: "Would you be content to be held close and treated tenderly and forget about 'the act'? Reply YES or NO and please add one line: 'I am over (or under) 40 years of age.' No signature is necessary." Even discounting for the fact that the disgruntled find more time to write than the contented, the percentage of those replying to Landers' inquiry who deemed themselves to be sexually burdened was impressive. More than 70 percent replied YES and 40 percent of those affirmatives were under 40 years of age. Clearly the people who find sex to be a burden transcend the boundaries of the British Isles. Over 90,000 letters poured in from the U.S. and other places where Landers' column appears (in Canada, Europe, Tokyo, Hong Kong, Bangkok, Mexico). This outpouring has exceeded every inquiry that Landers has directed to her readers, except for the pre-fab letter to be sent to President Reagan on the subject of nuclear war. "This sex survey beats . . . the poll asking parents, 'If you had to do it over again, would you have children?'" (Seventy percent said NO.) (Some astute historians of religion have argued that Manichaeaism persists as the ranking heresy in the West.)

Critics of the Landers report have warned that her results are not scientific. Her respondents are self-selective and her question tips the responses negatively. By placing the term for intercourse in quotation marks and calling it "the act," she tends to separate the sex act from tenderness. Still, the grammar of her question does not force an either/or response: tenderness or sex. However parsed, Landers uncovers a great deal of dissatisfaction amongst women . . . "it's a burden, a bore, no satisfaction . . ." Her letter-writers largely blame men for this state of affairs, but her survey and the ensuing discussion leave untouched the question as to whether the male failure to satisfy reflects a deeper masculine version of the experience of sex as a nuisance. One thinks here not of the occasionally impotent male who is agonizingly aware of sex as a nuisance, but, of the robust stallion who prides himself on his efficient performance but who finds foreplay, afterplay, tenderness, and gratitude an incomprehensible and burdensome detail.

THEOLOGICAL INTERPRETATION

Since I am a trained Protestant theologian, not a social commentator, I will close with a few comments about each of these four attitudes on the basis of the biblical tradition. In these matters I don't think I stray too far from what my colleagues in the rabbinate and priesthood might say.

1. Whatever criticisms the biblical tradition might deliver against the casualist approach to sex, that approach has an element of truth to it. Not all sexual encounter should carry the weight of an ultimate significance. Sometimes sex is merely recreational, a way to fall asleep, a *jeu d'esprit,* to say nothing of a *jeu de corps.* But at the same time, the interpretation of a particular episode should not exhaust the full meaning of the activity. At first glance, the ideology of the casualist seems virile, optimistic, and pleasure-oriented. But a latent melancholy pervades it. The fantasy of transient pleasure as an interpretation of the full meaning of the act requires a systematic elimination of everything that might shadow the fantasy. The sacred grove trivializes into a playpen. Hugh Hefner's original policy of never accepting a story for his magazine on the subject of death betrays the pathos of the approach. The fact of human frailty and death shatters the illusion upon which Hefner's world depends. By comparison, a sturdy optimism underlies a tradition that invites a couple to exchange vows that can stretch across the stark events of plenty and want, sickness and health, until death parts them. Since life is no playpen, it lets the world as it is flood in upon the lovers in the very content of their pledge.

Further, the casual outlook tends to ignore the inevitable complications of most sexual relationships. It lapses into a kind of emotional prudery. We are inclined to apply the word prudish to those who deny their sexual being. The modern casualist, however, is an emotional prude; that is, he tries to deny those emotions that cluster around his sexual life: affection, but not affection alone, loneliness in absence, jealousy, envy, preoccupation, restlessness, anger, and hopes for the future. The emotional prude dismisses all these or assumes that sincerity and honesty provide a kind of solvent that breaks down chemically any and all inconvenient and messy feelings: You hope for the future? But I never promised you a future. Why complain? I am emotionally clean, drip-dry. Why not you? This antiseptic view overlooks the element of dirt farming in sex and marriage. Caesar ploughed her and she cropped. Put another way, this view overlooks the comic in sex; adopting the pose of the casual it lacks a comic sense. It overlooks the way sex gets out of control. Sex refuses to stay in the playpen. It tends to defy our advance formulae. It mires each side down in complications that need to be respected.

If sex is a great deal more important, complicated, and consequential for the destiny of each partner than the committed casualists are wont to pretend, then it may not be out of place to subject it to a deliberateness, to submit it to a discipline, to let sexual decisions be *decisions* instead of resolving sexual ties by the luck of the draw, opportunity, and drift. The Hebrew tradition emphasized and symbolized the element of deliberateness in sexual life when it imposed the rite of circumcision. The rite does not deny the natural (as castration does with a vengeance) but neither does it accept the natural vitalities without their conforming to purposes that transcend them. Human sexual life is properly itself only when it is drawn into the self's deeper identity. Thus, against those who reduce sex to the casual, the tradition says sex is *important,* and should be subjected to discipline like anything important and consequential in human affairs.

2. The approach of the dualists to sex, either those who elevate it to a transcendental evil or those who reduce it to a doggish burden, hold to an element of truth. Sometimes, sexual activity can be abysmally self-destructive and destructive of others; at other times, it is merely a burdensome obligation. But, from the biblical perpective, both approaches wrongly estimate sexual love: they confuse the abuse of an activity with the activity itself. Sexual love is a good rather than an evil. God created man in his own image, *male and female* created He them. Genesis provides quite an exalted theory of sexual identity. Not divine, but in the image of God.

This differing estimate of sexual love shifts dramatically the meaning and warrants for discipline in one's sexual life. The Manichaeans disciplined sexual activity in the sense that they sought to eradicate it altogether; they justified radical denial on the ground that sex is inherently *evil.* The Jew and Christian, on the other hand, justify discipline on the basis of the goodness of sexual power.

Unfortunately, most popular justifications of discipline, especially in the perspective of the young, rest on the evilness of an activity or a faculty. Discipline the child because he is evil. Renounce your sexuality because it corrupts. This is the Manichaean way.

We may need to recover the vastly more important warrant for discipline that we already recognize in education and that the biblical tradition largely supports. The goodness and promise of the human mind, not its evilness, justifies the lengthy discipline of an education. Because the child has worthwhile potentialities, we consider it worth our while to develop her to the maximum. Because the piano is a marvelously versatile and expressive instrument, we think it worth the labors of the talented person to realize the full potentialities of the instrument rather than trivialize its capabilities with "Chopsticks." Some sexual encounters are not so much wicked as trivial, less than the best.

3. Finally, the sex-mystics also have an element of truth on their side. The event of sexual intercourse does supply us with one of our privileged contacts with ecstasy—the possibility of being beside ourselves, of moving beyond ourselves, experiencing a level of energy and urgency that both suspends and restores the daily round. But when all is said and done, sexuality, though a good, is only a *human* good, not *divine* as such. Despite Lawrence's perorations on the subject of love and the mountains atremble for Robert Jordan and his mate in Hemingway's *For Whom the Bell Tolls,* the act of sexual intercourse falls short of Exodus–Mount Sinai, death-resurrection. Intercourse is not an event of salvation; neither is marriage another name for redemption.

Biblical realism requires us to acknowledge three ways of abusing sex—to malign it with the dualists, to underestimate it with the casualists, but also to overestimate it with the sentimentalists and therefore to get angry, frustrated, and retaliatory when it fails to transcend the merely human. As a sexologist, St. Augustine had his faults, but he recognized that people tend to engage in a double torture when they elevate the human into the divine—whether it be sex, marriage, children, or any other creaturely good.

First, they condemn themselves to disappointment; they torture themselves. If men and women look for the resolution to all their problems in marriage, if they look to it for salvation, they are bound to discover that neither sex nor marriage converts an ordinary human being into someone sublime. They let themselves in for a letdown. Second, one not only tortures oneself, one also tortures the partner to whom one has turned. One places on the mate too heavy a burden. Dostoevsky tells of a dream in which a driver flogs a horse, forcing it to drag an overloaded wagon until the horse collapses under too much weight. We similarly overburden another when we look to him for too much. We expect others to function as a surrogate for the divine. Thus parents drive their thwarted ambitions through their children like a stake through the heart. Some marriages break up not because people expected too little from marriage, but because they have expected too much.

This biblical realism need not produce the sort of pessimism that expects little of the world and savors even less. Indeed, it should free us a little for enjoyment. Once we free our relationships to others from the impossible pressure to rescue us or redeem us, perhaps we can be free to enjoy them for what they are. Specifically, we can enjoy without shame and with delight a sexual relationship for the pleasurable, companionable, and fertile human good that it is.

Love and the Limits
of Individualism

WILLARD GAYLIN

It may be startling, if not wrong-headed, to find a volume
devoted to understanding the complexity of passionate attachments where the chapter on the nature of love is authored
by a psychoanalyst, while the chapter on the nature of sex is
written by a Christian theologian. Surely it should be the reverse: love is at the heart of Christian philosophy, as sexual
drive is the core of Freudian psychoanalytic theory. Beyond
the perverse desire of experts to speak on subjects of which
they know little, there may be a reasonable explanation.

The theologian Daniel Williams has stated:

> Before we go further we must look at one of the perplexities in
> all discussions of love. English has one word for love. Greek has
> at least four. In the vocabulary of love we can distinguish between
> epithemia, desire, often with the connotation of impurity or lust:
> eros, which is love of the beautiful, the true and the good, the
> aspiration for fulfillment of the soul's yearning; filia, brotherly

This essay is an abbreviated argument which in its fuller form is published as *Rediscovering
Love*, Willard Gaylin, M.D. (New York: Viking Press, 1986).

love which can mean either the comradely and affectionate love of brother and friends, or the ethical love of neighbor; and agape, which in Greek can be used for most of the loves, but in the New Testament is the redeeming love of God.[1]

Only agape, the love of God, was worthy of the designation "love" in early Christian philosophy. To suggest that even the Platonic and pure feelings between human beings devoid of all sexual connotation could be considered "love" was to risk heresy. Yet, by the middle ages church scholars were becoming infused with a Platonic extension of love that was to include love of our fellows, since after all they are the products of God's creative powers, and in honoring them with this feeling we are merely extending our love of God to His works. And while the Neoplatonists of the Renaissance came dangerously close to introducing a physical component to love, the sexual component was for generations excluded from acknowledgment, let alone serious analysis in treatises of love. But how can love possibly—in this modern post-Freudian day—be adequately examined without some consideration of its connections to, derivations from, and contradictions with sexual desire? The Christian theologian must reexamine today, as did each generation of his predecessors, the central tenet of his religion in terms of the definitions, the "realities" of his time. He must attend to the role of sex in human relationships.

In a pathetically contrary manner the traditional psychoanalyst has chosen to live in a loveless theoretical world. Sex was everything. Friendship, creativity, work, and beauty were simply sublimations and reaction formations, derivatives, and disguised forms of our instinctually driven animal sexuality. And God was reduced to an illusion.

But the modern psychoanalyst has suffered the misfortune of surviving the victory of his philosophy (the triumph of the therapeutic) and must now suffer the humiliation of living in this unlovely world that is in great part of his own creation. While the final score is not yet in, the results of the sexual revolution so far are less than reassuring. The liberation of the sexual drive from the repressive forces of a Puritanical environment has brought no surcease from neurotic anxiety and despair. The loveless world of casual sexuality is surely not the healthy environment to which we aspired. Surely, Freud, of all people, understood the role of human imagination in shaping human experience. He was a product and a part of the broad tradition of German idealism, and as such the world as it actually existed was less important in the psychic affairs of the human being than the world perceived. Surely even human appetites are influenced by the human imagination. Sex cannot be the automatic and animalistic mechanism described in the libido theory; pleasure cannot simply be the energic product of released sexual tension. Sex must be placed somewhere, somehow, into its proper position within a broader, more sophisticated concept of "attachments" and— yes—love.

THE PLEASURE PRINCIPLE

In his early research, Freud had focused on the interaction between the individual and his environment. He postulated a theory of the traumatic development of neurosis; an individual became neurotic as a product of some specific experiences in his early environment which were aberrant and pathology-inducing. These traumata of childhood were to be defined as exclusively sexual. The child through seduction was forced into a damaged and vulnerable state which would be reactivated in adult life and result in a neurotic symptom.

Such a theoretical framework would have inevitably forced Freud to deal with the complex interactions between the various players in this drama. It would have brought to the forefront the *inter*personal—rather than just the *intra*personal—aspects of human behavior. Such a formulation when elaborated would have demanded a theory of emotions and a proper consideration of love.

Through a complicated set of reevaluations of data, self-analysis, and reconsiderations, Freud abandoned the traumatic theory of the formulation of neuroses. He decided that the source of pathology was to be found in the complicated dynamics of the internal life of the individual, and was strongly vested in genetic components. The individual was driven by a motivating force that was in great part instinctually fixed and determined. Originally this was conceived of as a dual force, consisting of two instincts—one serving survival of the group, and the other serving survival of the individual. Eventually, Freud fused the two into the concept of the libido, a sexual force which managed through its reproductive end to serve group survival and through orgastic pleasure to serve individual motivation.

The "libido theory" then became a uni-instinctual theory seeing all behavior as products of the driving force of the sexual instinct and of the counterforces that kept it in check. The environment and the events of the child's experience had meaning only as they were internalized, and as they could influence the vicissitudes of the libido. The *intra*personal life of the person was to become the exclusive focus of the psychoanalysts. Conflict became the central thesis, and intrapsychic conflict at that. It was a world of forces and counterforces (psychodynamics), and the emotions were incidental fallout and ultimately scientifically uninteresting. The attachments were neglected as we charted the topology and the structure of our struggles with our only important adversaries—ourselves. We had, without his eloquence, anticipated Pogo and discovered the enemy in ourselves. In a world in which relationships are secondary phenomena and emotions are derivative, love will never be discovered.

All attention was placed on the instinctual drive and the counterforces that contained it. Pleasure was defined strictly in terms of sexual release; pain in terms of sexual frustration. It was a model built on a hydraulic principle more suitable for explaining the mechanisms of urination and bladder function than the complex subject of human pleasure and human motivation. This drive for instinctual (sexual) gratification was labelled the pleasure principle, and for a preponderant time in psychoanalytic theory was the sole motivating force by which all human behavior was presumed to be driven. It was a hedonic view of life, seeing the human species as driven by the need for sexual gratification, controlled by civilization and its constraints and by certain ill-defined counterforces within human nature.

But what of those counterforces which created the dynamic tension out of which neuroses were born? Well, they were confusing, and—unfortunately—never adequately analyzed by

Freud. And that is too bad, for it is in the counterforces that we find the binding elements of the social being: the conscience mechanisms, unselfishness, the emotions and, finally, love.

The definition of pleasure in this pleasure principle was simplistic and peculiarly negativistic. Pleasure cast in terms of the relief of tension may be a perfectly suitable definition when we are speaking of animals hedonically regulated at a subcortical level. But the human cortex informs and modifies all activities that involve conceptualization. The concepts of pride, aesthetic sensibility, and fantasy—to name but a few with which Freud had both cognizance and interest—will never be explicable according to so limited and mechanistic a definition of pleasure.

Of course there is a pleasure in the satiation of hunger, and of course there is pleasure in orgastic release, but I doubt that anyone today would want to confine so complex a phenomenon as human pleasure to the limited area defined by the libido theory. Since the feeling of love is, in my mind, the highest form of human pleasure (albeit more than that), in order to understand the nature of love from a psychoanalytic point of view it is necessary to reevaluate and expand the concept of pleasure.

Pleasure Beyond the Pleasure Principle

The libido theory, despite its faults, provided such a stunning framework on which to construct a concept of human behavior, both normal and pathological, that it concentrated the attention of psychoanalysts from that point forward. The libido theory had at its heart a hedonic principle: the pursuit of pleasure and, by implication, the avoidance of pain; but it was a limited concept of pleasure—the pleasure of instinctual release; and, indeed, a limited concept of pain—the frustration of instinctual release. The model that Freud presented—the emotional model—would be identical for man and for lower animals. This ignores the fact that human pleasure is a complicated amalgam of emotions operating at different levels.

Of course, the practicing psychoanalyst was aware of the power and diversity of human emotional responses, but nowhere was this incorporated into the theory as a crucial motivating factor in human behavior. A full theory of emotions is only now beginning to be developed in the psychoanalytic community. Space will not allow any comprehensive discussion here of the complexity of human pleasure, but any understanding of love demands some awareness of the vast scope of the human emotional life.

Feelings and emotions are obviously not essential to animal survival. There are organisms that do quite well without any of these. It is unlikely that the amoeba has any feelings, yet I suspect that the probability for survival of the amoeba is greater than that for the human race. The amoeba operates under a simple mechanism. It will attempt to ingest anything nearby. If it is indeed digestible, so be it; if it is not, it is repelled. There is no need to conceive of emotions or even feelings there.

As one ascends the level from the lowest animal form, one sees the emergence of feelings of pain and pleasure, although I am reluctant to call these emotions. Pain is something to be avoided and pleasure something to be sought. It is conceivable that at one time there was a mutation which was anhedonic, that is, an animal form that loved toxins and loathed nutrients. That unfortunate individual could not have survived past the first mutation to create a new species.

So at one level of conception an "emotion" occurs at a very primitive and early level, if one is prepared to call this kind of pain and this kind of pleasure emotion. "True" emotions, or perhaps a more accurate term would be complex emotions, demand the presence of distance receptors: some mechanisms of sight, audition, smell, or even the capacity to sense vibrations. To examine the distinction between emotions and sensations a crude example I have used in the past will suffice.

Without distance receptors but with a nervous system that integrated pain one would be aware of the survival danger when one felt the bite of the predator and experienced pain, but by the time the alligator has his teeth firmly entrenched into your lower limb the pain serves survival minimally if at all. If, however, one is capable of seeing the alligator in the distance, or smelling him, or hearing him, one can identify the predator at a time when escape is still possible.

By "identify" I do not mean an anthropomorphic capacity

to conceptualize something as "alligator" or even "predator." Probably at the simplest level the alligator smell directly generates the emotion of fear which directly initiates the action of flight.

Distance receptors, therefore, enhance survival by buying time and are mediated by emotions of fear or, if the predator can be attacked and demolished, rage. Fear and rage are survival mechanisms which not only provide us the feelings (the warnings that alert us), but simultaneously initiate the physiological preparations for fight or flight. They, of course, do many other things.

In group animals, and Homo sapiens is such, feelings are contagious. The expression of feelings, the demonstrable sense of fear or rage in one member, mobilizes the herd, the group, or the family to similar feelings and protective actions. Emotions, then, are powerful motivators of behavior providing an edge on survival. These simple survival emotions we share with many lower and less elevated species than our own.

When in addition to emotions a species has the kind of refined intelligence possessed by the human species you need not even wait for the distance receptors to pick up the presence of danger. One need not wait for the actual smell or sight of the alligator. One simply learns by experience not to walk in swamps at night. Magically that experience may never have been experienced by you or even your contemporaries, but rather have been communicated to you through the wonder of language. Knowledge combined with intelligence, cognition, and imagination can allow for the avoidance of dangerous places, the discovery of weapons of defense, the building of shelter, and the structuring of our defenses in such a way as to support our survival.

This crude and insensitive abbreviation of the evolution of emotions will at least serve to introduce the idea of emotions as species and individual survival functions. They are adaptive tools. We learn, therefore, to trust our emotions.[2]

Yet even in the limited area of emotions (forgetting the nature of human intelligence for the moment) the human species is unique unto itself. We do not just possess the emergency emotions of fear and rage. We have pride, shame, guilt, and something called love which while tied to passion is more complicated and subtle. What is the survival value of these sensitive, caring, and often self-sacrificing emotions? How can guilt and shame or empathy and love, with the self-denial or self-punishment they will often lead to, serve a "survival mechanism"? This is best understood by examining another unique aspect of human development.

The human animal is born in a state of helplessness unparalleled in the animal kingdom, and it will remain in a state of total incapacity to survive for a longer period of its existence than any other complex creature. If one thinks of dependency in terms of being able to survive on one's own and sustain the species, one must go up to age fourteen or fifteen, a quarter or a fifth of the life-expectancy of the pre-civilized human. If you add to this considerations of economic survival, and the complex technological world in which we live, we have extended the age of dependency well into the thirties. But the guppy when first born has only one immediate purpose for survival, and that is to swim like the devil to avoid being devoured by its mother, who in her postpartum state sees the guppy simply as a delicacy to satisfy her needs. The human infant on the other hand is capable of neither fight nor flight. It has substituted clutch and cling and must assume a loving adult to support its defenselessness.

The reason for this seemingly maladaptive and prolonged dependency—this extra-uterine period of attachment to parents—is a result of some peculiarities in our evolution: our profound capacity for intelligence, and our adoption of an upright posture. The human brain is massive, but the human pelvis, formed by the need to have an upright state, cannot accommodate to the fully formed head. A baby's brain at birth weighs three hundred and fifty grams. This in itself is an unparalleled percentage of the birth weight, but it grows to eight hundred and twenty-five grams by the end of the first year, and by the end of the second year the baby's brain will weigh one thousand grams out of a total adult expectancy of fourteen hundred! This huge brain simply cannot get out of the birth canal unless the child is born "prematurely." This explains why some neonatologists have described the first year of life as an extra-uterine fetal year.

What then sustains this helpless "fetus" during its stage of dependency? The caring attitude of the adults toward the child is the uterus and placenta of the extra-uterine life. One must presume an in-built and genetically fixed sense of caring—not one that is discovered or learned—for the helpless fetus not just on the part of the mother but from all members of the adult community. Certainly it is easy enough to assume a maternal caring attitude, but paternal protection, let alone general "love" or concern toward the newborn by the adult community, seems more problematic. Still one must recognize that in the million or more years of human existence, the concept that copulation was directly related to childbirth is a recent discovery, perhaps going back twenty or twenty-five thousand years. Even in modern times there have been discovered primitive societies which would not accept or did not understand the concept of paternity. Nonetheless, on those cold wintry days in the caves of precivilization, neither the male nor other adult members of the clan perceived the newborn children as delicate substitutes for hunting and foraging. If they had, there would never have evolved this extraordinary, exasperating, this peculiar species, this "upright ape."

It is this prolonged dependency which telologically demands an assumption of a whole range of caring and unselfish emotions on the part of the adult community towards the helpless. This can often extend beyond just the fetal. Rene Dubois in a touching anecdote analyzes the discovery of a prehistoric skull of a congenitally blind, *old* human and makes the point that no skull of any other species could be so discovered. Only the human species would support a congenitally blind individual into old age.[3]

Recent research has lent empirical support to the logically deduced view of human nature as being endowed with care and compassion. This greater understanding of the genetic nature of human caring and maternal love has emerged most dramatically in the last twenty to thirty years from studies in neonatology. I recommend to you the works of Klaus and his group in rediscovering not only the presence of maternal "instincts" but the mechanisms of their initiation.[4]

Freud, that most brilliant of observers, was aware of the biological directives for love, at least late in his life and when he attempted that massive reevaluation of his theories in the

1920s. In what may be his greatest piece of late analytic theoretical writing—*Inhibitions, Symptoms and Anxiety,* Freud discussed the two crucial factors in human development, one psychological, and the other biological:

> The biological factor is the long period of time during which the young of the human species is in a condition of helplessness and dependence. . . . this biological factor then establishes the earliest situation of danger and creates the *need to be loved* [italics mine] which will accompany the child through the rest of its life.[5]

Why did it take Freud so long to deal with the "need to be loved"? And why did he never extend beyond the need into some theory of the obligatory capacity to *give* love or to care for others, when surely these are as essential ingredients for human survival, dictated by the same observations and reasoning? It was certainly not because he was unaware of a strange set of emotions which seemed to be self-defeating and, therefore, inconsistent with his instinctual view of a self-serving drive. It may be worth a slight historic discursion to trace Freud's ambiguities about the unselfish emotions.

In that work which many consider the birthplace of modern psychoanalysis, *Studies of Hysteria,* Breuer and Freud evolved a theory of neurosis that saw as its core the entrapment or encapsulation of an idea in an "unconscious."[6] This model, not terribly dissimilar from the idea of a foreign body forming an abscess, led to techniques for understanding behavior in terms of visiting the patient's past, and for curing neurosis by releasing the encapsulated ideas. But why were ideas trapped in the unconscious? And what was the mechanism and what was the purpose of the unconscious? Here, one sees in this dually authored work the distinction between talent and genius.

Breuer assumed that when a person was in a diminished state of consciousness, a disturbing thought could enter into the unconscious by slipping past the laggard guardianship of consciousness. Freud was dissatisfied with the accidental and therefore essentially unscientific nature of these encapsulated ideas. He was reluctant to place at the center of his theory of hysteria so undynamic and incidental a factor as a state of altered consciousness at the time the idea occurred. He conceived the concept of "repression" which was to be the first of many ego-defense mechanisms and a fundamental tenet of dynamic psychiatry—that is, a psychiatry which visualizes all human behavior in terms of forces and counterforces.

Freud insisted that an idea could not accidentally enter the unconscious but was repressed, pushed, if you will, into the unconscious because it was unacceptable. But what makes an idea unacceptable? And what was the counterforce against this drive for gratification? They were, Freud surprisingly stated, the emotional responses elicited by the thoughts, and he labelled them disgust, shame, and loathing.

At that time Freud had no idea where these moral forces came from. He simply enunciated them, assuming them as a part of the human condition. In so doing he implicitly recognized a moral genetic nature to the human being and a range of emotions in the service of that morality, painful and distasteful, that demanded the renunciation of purely selfish pleasure. Again it is not possible to demonstrate the scope of Freud's concern with these counterforces. It should be noted, however, that throughout his lifetime he attempted to understand these seeming contradictions to his principle of an instinctive pleasure-driven organism.

In 1905, ten years after the appearance of *Studies of Hysteria,* Freud successfully sidestepped the issue with the publication of the libido theory, presenting a mechanism for the avoidance of the caring emotions that was to serve modern psychoanalysis to the present. He stated that the human being was motivated by pleasure inherent in the gratification of the sexual drive. The pleasure of orgastic release was the exclusive fuel that motivated all behavior. All forces somehow or other emanated from that energy. He subsumed in a complicated set of reasoning that the "countercathexis" were, if analyzed carefully, merely derivatives of that same selfish emotional drive. The countercathexis, then, were all of those forces that tended to allow for a civilized world through the inhibition of our own selfish pursuit of our sexual hungers and tensions.

Throughout the remainder of his life Freud tinkered with the questions and challenges to his theory presented by love and altruism, but the libido theory nonetheless remained the centerpiece of his psychology. In *Civilization and Its Discontents* he concluded that there must be cultural forces emanating from civilization that keep our drives in check, never completely considering the illogicality of how a creature so designed ever survived to that *point of culture*.[8]

The central core of psychoanalytic theory never again systematically approached the emotions central to loving, tenderness, and caring. Freud, nonetheless, was haunted by the idea, and in his attempts to solve problems of culture—as distinguished from those of individual pathology—he repeatedly returned to the cohesive forces of unselfish behavior.

The first full treatment of something that might be thought of as a conscience mechanism occurs in a long-neglected and misunderstood volume called *Totem and Taboo,* published in 1912.[9] The paper is underappreciated because Freud, in sharing the ignorance of his day, had assumed a Lamarckian (as distinguished from Mendelian) mechanism of inheritance. If one strips this work of its faulty genetics and biology, its message emerges as sparkling and creative. Freud conceives of a relatively autonomous and independent set of behavior-controlling and impulse-limiting mechanisms—taboos as he called them—that were part of the genetic endowment of the species. These limitations and restrictions on the selfish pursuit of the sexual instinct are as much an inherent and genetical part of the species as the instinct itself. With this theory, social living, community, love and unselfishness become, not an accident of a culture that by sheer luck managed to control our destructive drives for pleasure, but part of our nature.

Totem and Taboo, then, defines the *group* as a genetic fact of life, and in so doing forces a new view of humanity in which love, compassion and care are inherent attributes. It pictures the group—the supporting network—as the true boundary of personhood. No more can the psychological unit be the individual, but the individual and his network of other supportive individuals. Conscience, love, self-sacrifice, unselfishness are also in the service of survival because human survival is finally understood in terms of a network of other people. In our own potentially precatastrophic time of unlimited nuclear capacity and capabilities of self-destruction, it is an urgent point worth recalling. It is to our selfish purpose, not to our unselfish purpose, to support the community at large.

Having said all this, psychoanalysis blithely continued in its operational framework to treat the sick person who was its constituent as an individual suffering from internal conflicts relatively independent of the real world that existed around him.

There is a theory of pleasure, therefore, waiting to be expounded that goes beyond the pleasure principle. There is a pleasure inherent in the human being that goes beyond instinctual gratification. The synthesis of a new concept of pleasure would bring with it the greatest justification for a central principle of love and loving.

There is in our species not only "the need to be loved" as Freud expressed it, but its corollary, the need to love. It is my thesis that the ultimate pleasure—a peculiar pleasure that involves pain, self-sacrifice, agony, guilt, shame, etc.—is the pleasure of loving as distinguished from being loved. Freud never discovered the nature of love because he was trapped in a limited concept of pleasure. If one attempts to find papers dealing with the subject of love in Freud, the irony is that those papers titled "Essays on the Understanding of Love" are in fact papers on male impotence. But Freud, in retrospect, was closer to a concept of true love than he might have imagined. The real question which persists is why in the fifty years of post-Freudian psychoanalysis a full blown attempt at consideration of love has not yet been attempted.

The neglect of emotion was almost inevitable, given the nineteenth century model of medicine from which it emerged. This neglect was further enhanced with the development of the libido theory and its enchantment with the primitive nineteenth century concept of energy. Determined to establish the fixed nature of the human being (ironically one major distinction in homo sapiens is the absence of such fixity), it spent its time studying the disposition of instinctual energy, at the same time neglecting the emotional counterparts. Reluctantly, however, psychoanalysis was forced to come to deal with emotions, but even then they were the darker emotions of rage and fear rather than of tenderness and caring.

It was through the necessity to understand adequately the depraved and destructive guilt that exists in clinical depression that psychoanalysis was precipitated into an awareness of the mechanism of identification, a concept that was to revolutionize modern psychoanalysis. Identification is not love but it is halfway there. That was as close as psychoanalysis was to come.

Identification and its counterpart mechanism of introjection (an idea of symbolically swallowing up someone for purposes of identifying with them) became—not by chance—the central features in Freud's concept of a conscience or superego. Since it is the conscience that binds us one to another, and conscience that prohibits our indulging our more venal and primitive instinctual urges, conscience becomes the instrument of concern, empathy, compassion and self-denial that again, while still not love, encompasses the components of love that were not easily understood in the early instinctual theories.

Through his study of the superego and his study of depression, Freud gradually developed a sophisticated concept of identification that tied one individual to another in a metaphoric bond of unity that was to be his alternative to love. One introjects a model of a mother or father figure and in internalizing this figure fuses one's own identity with the "introject" so that the individual, unaware of the unconscious process, finds difficulty distinguishing where the introject ends and the self begins. In other words, a little boy behaves like his father in many ways, not because his father instructed him step by step on how to walk, how to talk, how to think, and how to feel, but because in swallowing up this parental figure he "identifies with him" and learns through a wholesale mechanism to be, to become, and to respond like the introjected parent.

Post-Freudian psychoanalysis acknowledged that identification was a process that need not be restricted to the parents nor, for that matter, to the first few years of life.[10] Still, identification and fusion were seen as in the service of self-identity and these concepts were not extended to explain attachments and relationships. These unfortunately were still "explained" almost exclusively in terms of libidinal cathexes. Identity became a centerpiece of the new ego-analysis, and relationship was left behind in the sterile field of instinctual theory. But identity and relationship are integrally related phenomena, and through a renewed interest in transference (the relationship between patient and therapist in treatment) we are beginning to expand the concepts of identification and fusion.

Having established clearly the biological underpinnings of human behavior, as all good Freudians and physicians must do, let me now turn more directly to the cultural, to which all good psychologists and sociologists must attend. The leap is not as abrupt as some modern (and often politically inspired) debate would have one think. There need be no nature–nurture controversies here. There is almost nothing that involves a normal human being (and in dealing with love we are dealing with normal aspects of behavior) that is not modified by our culture. That statement does not mitigate the power of our biological endowments, for the fact that we are so vulnerable to cultural directives is itself a product of our idiosyncratic nature. We are the least instinctually-fixed of all species. Let me briefly comment on two broad aspects of the uniqueness of our species: the nature of our imagination, and the variable and modifiable nature of our nature.

By designating Freud as an idealist, I have already suggested the psychoanalytic awareness of the powers of the human imagination. Short of the extreme of starvation or other conditions at the fringe of survival, perception is everything to the human being. We are what we think we are; we are treated the way we think we deserve; and ultimately we define the actual world we will inhabit on the basis of the reality we anticipate. We can create a culture that enhances or reduces any aspect of our biological perspectives, including—unfortunately—even those most crucial for the survival of our species. I have made the case for caring as a biological imperative. But we know that there are brutal parents who neglect and torture their children. For the most part they have been "taught" to do so. Battering parents were either battered children, or severely deprived ones. Their "culture" trained them to violate a most fundamental directive of human nature. The way in which that culture can be utilized to define and distort our sense of ourselves, the way we behave and what we become, are best appreciated in the current literature of the gender revolution, where we see how modifiable so biological a factor as gender is to changing cultural definitions. This, then, leads directly to that second aspect of human nature.

It is the nature of human nature to change our nature. We are created incomplete with the capacity to become, with our creators, the co-authors—as the Victorians liked to put it—of our own lives. Values and moral principles determine directions. They too are motivators of behavior. And they are again peculiar to our species. Adding yet another peculiarity, these values like all acquired knowledge are transmissible from one generation to another. All of these considerations indicate the mutability of biological directives under the power of culture. All the more reason, therefore, that we define the values implicit in psychoanalytic theory. The neglect of love was unintended, but was interpreted as a disastrous dismissal of the central role of love in human affairs.

The concepts of identification, as incorporated into the mechanism of the superego, has brought psychoanalysis to its closest approximation of love. When properly understood, love and the need to be loved will be seen as more powerful motivating forces in human behavior than the desire for sexual release. Love is not only an alternative to self-gratification, but by modifying the sense of self it allows unselfish behavior to serve self-interest. To love someone is to so fuse their identity with our own so that even self-satisfaction may involve service to the other. The concept of fusion, which hitherto has been reserved in psychoanalysis for pathological states, must be seen as an essential and normal aspect of loving.

The concept of identification brought Freud closer to that state of fusion which I see as normal, and brought psychoanalysis closer than it realized to a major tradition in the philosophical analysis of love. In the *Symposium,* Plato devotes himself to an exploration of the nature of love. Many theories are offered and Socrates dismisses them all while he himself perversely refrains from offering a superior or alternative theory to those presented. One of the theories is the myth of Aristophanes, in which what I would define as the fusion that is central to the destruction of ego boundaries that occurs in loving, is presented in a poetic metaphor.

Aristophanes proposed that at one time primeval man was round with four hands and four feet, back and sides forming a circle. But the human beings were insolent and the Gods would not suffer such arrogance. So Zeus punished them:

They shall continue to exist but I will cut them in two and then they will be diminished in strength and increased in numbers.

. . . Each of us when separated is but the indenture of a man having one side only like a flat fish, and he is always looking for his other half . . . and when one of them finds his other half . . . the pair are lost in an amazement of love and friendship and intimacy. . . . The intense yearning which each of them has towards the other does not appear to be in the desire of intercourse but of something else which the soul desires and cannot tell, and of which she only has a dark and doubtful presentiment. . . .

There's not a man among them when he heard this who would deny or who would not acknowledge that this meeting and melting in one another's arms, this becoming one instead of two, was the very expression of his ancient need. *And the reason is that human nature was originally one and we were whole, and the desire and pursuit of that whole is called love.*[11] [Italics mine.]

It is made clear in this myth that while intercourse is one intense, passionate form of such fusion it is not the essential mechanism. Rather, that mechanism is the rediscovering of the self in another. Any sophisticated concept of love must ultimately embrace this ancient concept. This, I submit, is where modern psychoanalysis joins the ancient myth. Love is a fusion, a blurring of identities, and it is a fixed part of our species needs.

In modern times we have avoided the subject of loving by assuming that being loved is the same, but of course it is not. Being loved is a passive phenomenon and a self-indulgent one. Loving is an active, giving, and, consequently a self-enhancing and enlarging action.

We are regressing to a culturally encouraged state of oral passivity. The concept of love that is harbored by most people these days is something called "true love." True love seems to imply that regardless of what one does or how one behaves, one will be adored and worshipped. One finds a peculiar and popular hunger to be loved not for what one does but for what one is, as though the doing can be separated from the being. It is part of a self-actualizing phenomenon that sees the self as an isolated and independent entity.

What is this concept of a self that must be loved for its own sake, and how did it emerge in our society? On close analysis there is only one counterpart that makes any sense. There is only one time in life where "what you are" is separable from "what you do," and that is the state of infancy. Here is a peculiar state indeed. What an ungenerous creature is the infant and what an unnatural relationship between the parent and the infant. The infant does little that would normally be defined as attractive. It wakes one in the middle of the night. It has no consideration for others' fatigue. It screams at the least provocation. It will urinate on you, vomit on your best clothes, destroy precious articles, torture your pet, frighten and intimidate you. It gives little. It drains our energy and commands our attention. And we adore it! The modern concept of being loved is nothing less than a desire to return to that passive state of infancy. It is not an accidental event that it is the prevailing motif of these narcissistic times. It is the essential problem of our culture.

We are the most individualistic of cultures. It has of course been our glory that we respected the individual in a way that such communitarian but authoritarian societies as the Soviet Union and Communist China could not. We have pressed individualism so far that we are beginning to pay a terrible price, but we are finally beginning to recognize its limits. In our pursuit of individual liberties we have destroyed the common good and are learning the sad but primitive biological fact that there is no such thing as an individual human being. We exist through our supporting networks and if we succeed in destroying all community, we will destroy all the individuals within it. The pursuit of love in the assumption that it is a pleasure that can be defined as exclusively within ourselves is a major perversion of modern everyday activity. The concept of a biologically complete individual human being is truly the myth of our time.

Beyond Pleasure

Up to this point my explanation of the absence of a psychoanalytic theory of love has been based on the inadequate definition of pleasure used as a model. There is a pleasure beyond the crude, animal hunger and orgasm instinct and the gratification construction of pleasure that is at the core of early psychoanalytic theory. There is pleasure beyond the pleasure principle. There is a pleasure in any expanded and enlarged sense of self, whether it comes through sensate pleasure, mastery, communion with nature or God, friendship, or ultimately through love. This definition of pleasure, unlike that incorporated in the libido theory, does not see pleasure and pain as polar phenomena. The highest forms of pleasure—think of creativity, for example—always involve pain. Surely love does.

Having said this, however, there remains the question of whether love can be encompassed within any definition of pleasure. Certainly it is a form of pleasure, but it is more than that. If love is more than a form of pleasure, or even something other than pleasure, it challenges another profound assumption of psychoanalysis. Must human motivation be understood totally within the context of a pleasure system? Are we truly hedonic animals? Are we only hedonic animals? Is all motivation to be understood in terms of instinctual gratification or pursuit of pleasure regardless of how complicated a definition we give to that term? I think not. Unquestionably, hedonic regulation operates in the control of some human behavior, but just as certainly, it does so less than in any other species. The genetic directives inherent in our species that drive our behavior are complex. These motivating forces can often transcend pleasure and even override our personal survival.

We know that we will endure extreme pain and suffer great sacrifice, even to the point of sacrificing life, for those we love. Of course there is a game, usually learned in the sophomore year at college, that denies the concept of an unselfish act. In the grand sophomoric tradition it equates self-sacrifice, duty, and responsibility as "your form of pleasure." To such sophistry there is no answer. Most of us, however, are clear in our understanding that there are times in which we behave in a way that denies us our own pleasure for the sake of other duties, other responsibilities, other commitments. We have seen such behavior in ourselves and we have observed it in others.

Even though the modish language of our time is to speak of rights rather than responsibilities, the thinking person acknowledges that the one cannot exist without the other. It is time to rediscover commitment. I have previously alluded to the limits of individualism. It is because we are reaching those limits that I believe we must reexamine responsibility and rediscover community. We must label the so-called self-actualization movements of recent years (EST and its ilk) for what they are. They are regressions to pleasure at the oral level of the passive infant. Instead we must rediscover the forces and institutions that bind us together. In this shrinking world of increased shortages and increased mutual capacity for self-destruction, our survival may depend on the rediscovery of responsibility and community.

We have only to look at the statistics of the sexual revolution to realize the unintended damage that has already occurred. In the Harlem ghettos a 70 percent illegitimacy rate, with over 50 percent of the children being born to teenagers, is a hemorrhage on the future vitality of a black community already debilitated by generations of deprivation and disaffection. I do not think we will ever return to a past in which the power of the family was valued to a point where legal dissolution was prohibited. I would not necessarily prefer that we do that, but surely we must recognize that we have come to a point where we must question the trivialization of marriage vows and of parental responsibility.

The distinguished English philosopher, Derek Parfit, feels that all marriages are now essentially trial marriages and should be so labeled. Parfit feels this was inevitable since he denies we have the capacity to make moral commitments. He is answered with some wit and elegance by Susan Mendus. She states: "It is bizarre to respond to 'Wilt thou love her, comfort her, honor her and keep her?' with 'Well, I'll try.' " She continues by saying, "The claim that the marriage vow is either impossible or improper is false. It is possible to commit oneself unconditionally because commitment is analogous to a statement of intention, not to a prediction or a piece of clarvoyance. . . . further, it is simply not true that I am helpless in circumstances in which I find my commitment wavering: This is because my principles will initially serve to modify my view of the opportunities which present themselves, so that I simply will not see certain things as constituting success because my principles are such as to exclude such things as being constituted of success."[12]

It is refreshing to hear anything these days that could suggest that there may be such things as commitment based on principle rather than on pleasure and that there may be a system of motivation and controls that go "beyond pleasure."

It is important that we reexamine the concept of mature love in terms of commitment as well as pleasure. At the same time, I recognize some inherent contradictions and antagonisms in preserving our traditional ideas of romantic love and passion while reintroducing respect for commitment and family. If we cannot understand the nature of commitment between two people how can we possibly understand the nature of commitment to larger groups? We are at a point of public safety that demands that we revive concepts of identification and fusion with larger groups. If we cannot even fuse with one person how will we ever learn to fuse our identity with the larger populations that are becoming increasingly necessary for our community's survival?

We must relearn the lessons of Aristotle. The human being is a political animal. He is an "obligate" social animal. I use that term in its biological sense. A human being requires others of its kind in the same way he requires food and oxygen for his survival, not for his pleasure. There is no such thing as a human being without the presence of other human beings. Our nature is such that we could not physically survive, or indeed if we did that which would survive when deprived of human contact would be less than human. As the Russian philosopher, Vladimir Solovyov, said at the turn of the century: "The meaning of human love is the justification and deliverance of individuality through the sacrifice of egoism."[13]

A true concept of love would then go beyond pleasure and recognize that this unique creature that is Homo sapiens is the least hedonically regulated of all animals; the most capable of remodelling—for good or bad—his essential nature; and the one animal in whom cognition may elaborate a sense of duties, responsibilities, social justice, and good, that allows even for the abandonment, when necessary, of all personal pleasure.

And, optimist that I am and will always remain, I suspect that when we are prepared to give up all pleasure for the moral life we will rediscover the true meaning of pleasure and the true meaning of love. We will have learned, as William James once pointed out, what the words 'good' 'bad' and 'obligation' severally mean. They mean no absolute natures, independent of personal support. They are objects of feeling and desire, which have no foothold or anchors in Being, apart from the existence of actually living minds.

Wherever such minds exist, with judgments of good and ill, demands upon one another, there is an ethical world in its essential features. Were all other things, gods and men and starry heavens, blotted out from the universe, and were there left but one rock with two loving souls upon it, that rock would have as thoroughly moral a constitution as any possible world which the eternities and immensities could harbor. It would be a tragic constitution, because the rock's inhabitants would die. But while they lived, there would be real good things and real bad things in the universe; there would be obligations, claims, and expectations; obediences, refusals, and disappointments; compunctions and longings for harmony to come again, and inward peace of conscience when it was restored; there would, in short, be a moral life, whose active energy would have no limit but the intensity of interest in each other with which the hero and the heroine might be endowed.[14]

An expanded concept of love may allow us to discover the unique pleasure in: the sharing of pleasure; the abandonment of pleasure; the liberation from self-interest; or the fusing of one's own interests with that of others.

Between Conventionality and Aggression: The Boundaries of Passion

OTTO F. KERNBERG

Until approximately twenty years ago, it seemed that psychoanalysis had much more to say about the pathology of sexual behavior than about the pathology of love relations. This situation has now changed radically. In what follows I briefly outline some of the contributions that have changed our perspective, deepened our understanding, and opened new roads for exploration in this important area.

The basic theoretical frames underlying these recent developments had all been formulated by Freud between 1905 and 1925.[1] Therefore, one might well ask what was responsible for the forty-year gap between Freud's contributions and the contemporary psychoanalytic exploration of love relations. I believe that the intimate connections between normal love life and passionate involvements, on the one hand, and pathology of sexual functions and of love relations, on the other, point to the delicate, fragile nature of normal love, blur the boundaries between patients' pathology and the analysts' life experience, and may have created a phobic attitude akin to that which delayed the study of countertransference until the early 1950s.

In briefly reviewing Freud's contributions and subsequent developments in the areas surrounding these contributions I attempt to provide a common frame for a description of the love life of the sexual couple. In this context I explore how contemporary formulations may help to clarify certain conflicts between conventional morality and the psychological reality of the couple in love.

INFANTILE SEXUALITY AND THE PERVERSIONS

Freud, in his "Three Essays on the Theory of Sexuality," proposed that the sexual drive originates from various sources that constitute component sexual instincts, and that these component sexual instincts codetermine the earliest stages of psychosexual development that culminate in the infantile genital stage. He pointed to the erotic functions of key body zones—the mouth, the anus, and the skin, in addition to the genital zones—and to the importance of the condensation of pleasurable and painful stimuli in sadistic and masochistic sexual excitement. Freud postulated a psychological bisexuality reflected in the coexistence of homosexual and heterosexual urges, voyeuristic and exhibitionistic urges expanding the eroticism linked with genital excitement, and the integration of all these tendencies in normal foreplay leading to sexual intercourse and orgasm. Freud thus highlighted one crucial component of passionate sexual love, namely, the integration of polymorphous "perverse" infantile sexual tendencies with genital excitement. The term "perverse" here is meant to indicate that these normal features also are the potential root of later sexual pathology, the perversions.

Although controversies persist within contemporary psychoanalytic views of this theory, I think that no serious challenge exists to my view of the importance of three factors:

1. The recognition of the importance of bodily stimulation in the first few years of life as part of a gratifying mother-infant relationship that permits kindling of skin eroticism. In

the absence of such kindling, at most severe levels of pathology of love relations, there, may develop not only an incapacity for longing and tenderness, but also an incapacity for erotic excitement, an incapacity that is not due to sexual repression and is prognostically grave.

2. The importance, in addition to libidinal components, of aggression in sexual play and intercourse, and of the activation of implicit homosexual excitement and gratification in the mutual identification that takes place as part of intercourse and orgasm.

3. The understanding that in these normal, polymorphous perverse fantasies and activities there is a symbolic activation of the earliest object relation of the infant with mother, and of the small child with both parents in fantasied activities that condense preoedipal and oedipal relations with them.

In earlier work, I proposed that the normal perverse components of sexual play and intercourse—such as fellatio, cunnilingus, anal penetration, as well as exhibitionistic, voyeuristic, sadistic, and masochistic sexual games—maintain their erotic intensity because they activate unconscious fantasies regarding the oedipal and preoedipal objects.[2] If, as is the case in narcissistic personalities, such internalized object relations deteriorate, the normal perverse sexual play also may deteriorate into mechanical activities that lose their erotic potential.

4. There is a growing awareness of the importance of these polymorphous perverse tendencies as part of normal love relations, in contrast to their subordination to genital intercourse. I have proposed that normal polymorphous perverse sexuality is an essential component that maintains the intensity of a passionate love relation, and recruits—in its function as the receptacle of unconscious fantasy—the conflictual relations and meanings that evolve in a couple's relationship throughout time. A corollary of this idea is that the traditional psychoanalytic view of perversions needs to be reexamined, and that the definition of perversion as a pathological psychological structure may have to be revised. I think perversions should be defined more narrowly as the obligatory, habitual restriction of sexual fantasies and activities to one particular sexual component.

5. Finally, insofar as sexual passion includes the freedom

of unconsciously integrating love and hatred in polymorphous sexual behavior, an implicit frame of a safe object relation of the couple needs to be maintained. This frame permits tolerating the playful use or "exploitation" of each other as part of sexual games, a regressive splitting of the self at the service of sexual excitement and love that enters into a dialectic contradiction with the opposite tendency that we shall examine next, namely, the urge for fusion experiences in the sexual object relation.

The Oedipal Structure: Direct and Reverse Triangulation in Love Relations

Freud proposed in "Three Essays" that infantile sexuality culminates in the dominance of genital impulses directed to the parent of the opposite sex, and the simultaneous activation of intense ambivalence toward and rivalry with the parent of the same sex. The development of unconscious parricidal or matricidal wishes to the parent of the same sex is a counterpart to the incestuous wishes for the parent of the other sex, and the fear of castration a corresponding unconscious fantasy of threatened punishment. This constellation, the positive Oedipus complex, is the counterpart of the negative Oedipus complex, that is, the sexual love for the parent of the same sex and a sense of rivalry and aggression directed at the parent of the opposite sex. The activation of the negative Oedipus complex as a defense against the castration anxiety activated by the positive Oedipus complex, in other words, a defensive homosexual submission, Freud considered an important but not exclusive motive for the negative Oedipus complex, the roots of which resided in preoedipal bisexuality.

This theory illuminated the nature of transference love, providing the explanation for the patient's intense attachment to the analyst as an ideal, unavailable, forbidden object. But Freud, astonished by the intensity and violence of transference love and its unmistakable relation to normal falling in love, concluded that the unconscious search for the oedipal object is part of all normal love relations and provides the undercurrent of the longings and idealization of the love object.[3] As M. S. Bergmann has pointed out, however, Freud never formulated a comprehensive theory of normal love and of falling in love that would clearly differentiate transference love from neurotic love and normal love.[4]

I believe romantic love, with its constituents of idealization, longing, and the sense of passionate fulfillment when the love relation with the desired object is achieved, reflects the unconscious achievement of the union with the desired incestual object and yet the capacity to overcome the infantile equation of all sexual objects with the oedipal one, and a triumphant identification with the oedipal rival without the implication of parricide or matricide. In normal passionate love, the distinction between the original oedipal rival and other competitors of the same sex has been achieved, and the related sense of inferiority to both parental objects linked with the infantile origin of the Oedipus complex has been overcome.

Sexual intercourse, under these conditions, represents the crossing of the boundaries that separate a man from a woman, an act of defiance which secretively ruptures unconscious oedipal prohibitions. Overcoming oedipal prohibitions is a profound source of sexual excitement and passionate love. Here, the love for the oedipal object and the triumph over the oedipal rival, the erotic excitement of sexual intimacy linked with the aggressive gratification of overcoming the secret, unavailable, and forbidden sexual barriers that separated the oedipal objects replay the condensation of love, eroticism, and aggression that we examined at the level of polymorphous perverse infantile sexuality.

In "A Special Type of Choice of Objects Made by Men," Freud described a prevalent type of pathology of love relations, wherein a man can tolerate a tender relation only with idealized women, and a purely erotic one with debased women. This pathological configuration derives from the incapacity to overcome the unconscious infantile prohibitions against incest and the need to protect the idealized love object from forbidden incestuous genital strivings. In both sexes, such a discrepancy between tender and genital love leads to frequent disturbances of the capacity for sustained love relations that reflect the persistence of unresolved oedipal conflicts.

Recent psychoanalytic thinking by D. Braunschweig and M. Fain has expanded and enriched this conceptualization, particularly regarding the different psychology of men and women, in that a woman is the first love object for both sexes, and that girls but not boys must change the incestuously loved object.[5]

Freud's theory, set forth in "Three Essays," that penis envy is the reason for the little girl's turning from mother to father—thus initiating the oedipal scenario—has recently been seriously questioned. Strong evidence suggests that the envy of the sexual organs of the other sex is an equally important anxiety for both sexes. Contemporary psychoanalytic thinking stresses the origin of penis envy in the little girl in preoedipal conflicts between mother and daughter, and the activation of intense aggression in the daughter and the displacement of that aggression on father in the form of penis envy.[6]

Evidence for early genital awareness in little girls, and its discouragement by mother, in a culture that in contrast fosters a little boy's pride in his penis, are other observations that raise questions regarding Freud's theory of penis envy. Braunschweig and Fain in *Eros and Anteros* have pointed to both the biological origins of the little girl's attachment to her father, and the psychological "act of courage" implied in changing the object of her love from mother to father. They link this act of courage with the hypothesis that women may be better prepared to establish stable relations than men because they have already given up their original love object on entering the oedipal phase.

Chasseguet-Smirgel described the little boy's fear that his small penis might not be sufficient to fulfill the sexual needs of mother as a powerful motivation for the little boy's abandonment of his rivalry with father, and for a defensive self-idealization that, under pathological circumstances, leads to a man's childlike narcissistic relation with women who have not come to terms with their oedipal longings for father and select an effeminate little boy-man in an unconscious collusion against the symbolic father's penis.[7]

In contrast to predominantly oedipal psychopathology reflected in the sexual conflicts mentioned so far, more severe narcissistic pathology in both sexes is related to intense envy of the preoedipal mother, unconscious preoedipal rage and fears displaced from mother onto the oedipal relationship, and a consequent sadomasochistic distortion of the fantasied sexual relation between the parents. This pathology is characterized by an intense penis envy and hatred of men in the case of narcissistic women, and an equally intense unconscious hatred of women in the case of narcissistic men that leads in both sexes to an incapacity for stable love relations in the context of unconscious devaluation of the love object. Conquering the love object makes it frustrating, indifferent, and boring, and causes a narcissistically determined sexual promiscuity.

Many narcissistic patients maintain their capacity for falling in love, but their capacity for remaining in love is seriously damaged. The unconscious devaluation of the love object explains the deterioration not only of love relations but also of the ungratifiable excitement with sexual activities per se that characterizes narcissistic personalities over the years. Sex may still remain exciting while novelty is preserved, but the destruction of the internalized world of object relations interferes with the stable deployment of normal polymorphous perverse sexual urges: sexual boredom reflects the loss of the unconscious fantasy life that underpins the perverse components of erotic excitement.

In addition to focusing on the intimate relation between oedipal and preoedipal conflicts as part of the reactivation of the oedipal complex in love relations, Bergmann under the influence of M. S. Mahler's contributions, has pointed to other issues involved in sexual passion. Insofar as the earliest attachment to mother occurs when the infant does not yet have a differentiated concept of the self or of mother, the wish to return to an experience of fusion with mother within an overall exciting, fully gratifying state of bliss may underly the passionate experience of sexual excitement and shared orgasm with a sexual partner.[8]

I have suggested in *Internal World and External Reality* that there is a basic, intrinsic contradiction between two crucial features of sexual love: the necessity for a self with firm boundaries, and a constant awareness of the separateness of others, contradicts the necessity for being able to transcend the boundaries of the self so as to become one with the loved person. Sexual passion integrates these contradictory features; the shared experience of orgasm includes the transcendence from the experience of the self into that of the fantasied union of the oedipal parents, as well as the transcendence of the repetition of the oedipal relation to an abandonment of it in a new object relation that reconfirms one's separate identity and autonomy.

An additional dimension of the capacity for passionate love derives from the work of British psychoanalysts, particularly W. D. Fairbairn and M. Klein; from the work of Mahler mentioned earlier; and from that of Jacobson in the United States.[9] Contemporary psychoanalytic thinking conceives of the early object relations that predate the oedipal stage of development as characterized by first, the earliest stage of lack of differentiation between self and object that Mahler described as the stage of symbiosis; second, a later stage of separation-individuation in which self- and object representations are differentiated from each other, but not yet integrated into a cohesive conception of self and others; and third, a still later phase in which self-representations under the impact of aggressive drive derivatives and self-representations under the impact of libidinal drive derivatives have been integrated into a global self concept that is able to tolerate or contain both love and hatred in the view of oneself as well as love and hatred in the perception of significant others. This is the phase of object constancy that inaugurates the oedipal period.

That integration of love and hatred, crucial for the establishment of object relations in depth and for the normal differentiation of the oedipal parents—including their sexual identity—from each other, implies the capacity for ambivalence; that is, the capacity to tolerate both love and hatred for a loved object. This tolerance of ambivalence is a crucial indicator of the capacity for differentiation in the evaluation of others; it permits, for example, a man to select one woman as different from all others, rather than to experience all women as equal because they have the same genitalia. This tolerance of ambivalence also prevents, at a severe level of psychopathology, equating all individuals of one sex as good, while all those of the other sex are considered bad.

In essence, then, the capacity for sexual passion for one of the other sex implies the tolerance for a symbolic refusion that reflects the remnants of original symbiosis; a consolidation of the self concept; the achievement of the capacity for ambivalence and, with it, of containment of aggression by love; and by the same token the repetition, at the level of the human relationship, of the integration of love and aggression in the context of normal polymorphous perverse sexuality.

One of the most interesting findings of contemporary psychoanalytic exploration has been the awareness of the universality and permanence of the oedipal constellation as an unconsciously structured fantasy that influences a couple's love relation throughout time, and that both threatens the couple as well as maintains the intensity of their love.[10] I am proposing now that there is a constant, latent tendency in each individual to experience himself or herself as part of a double triangle consisting, on the one hand, of the individual and his or her oedipal objects, and, on the other, of the individual and two representatives of the oedipal object of the other sex. Let us examine first the triangle formed by the individual and both oedipal objects. It is as if he or she were struggling constantly with an invisible, excluded third party who represents the oedipal rival.

In practice, fantasies that another person of the same sex as the individual would be sexually more effective, more attractive, more exciting, more fulfilling to the sexual partner are universal; and the fantasy that one's sexual partner is having sex with such a rival is a source of pain, but also, surprisingly enough, of sexual excitement as well. Fantasies during sexual intercourse about the partner's sexual involvement with a third party are frequently found in masochistic psychopathology, and among normal people as well; and the predisposition to intense jealousy and potential aggression against oedipal rivals is a powerful source of all other types of competitiveness in social life. Behind the fear of one's death and the fear of abandonment by one's partner is the fear of the triumph of the oedipal partner; and behind the unconscious tendency to provoke the loved object to infidelity is the challenge of the oedipal rival as well as the activation of the unconscious homosexual longing for that rival.

I am calling this "direct triangulation," and contrast it with "reverse triangulation," which has a reassuring and revengeful quality, and consists in fantasies of being involved with two persons rather than with one, most frequently expressed in fantasies during sexual intercourse of having intercourse with another person of the same sex as one's present sexual partner. This fantasy is, of course, the reverse of the original oedipal situation in which the little boy, for example, competed with father for mother. Now, in contrast, a man fantasies a relation with another woman, and the rivalry of two women fighting over him. Or a married woman requires a lover to feel assured of her sexual value and attractiveness and in order to be able to enjoy her sexual life with her husband.

This reverse triangulation, however, not only permits the enactment of the vengeful fantasy of having turned the table on the ambivalently loved oedipal parent, but, by threatening the boundaries of an exclusive love relation, it may also relieve unconscious guilt over the symbolic replacement of the parent of the same sex: an obviously less than perfect marriage can be better tolerated than a fully satisfactory one. In addition, such a triangular relation may render both a marital and an extramarital relation forbidden and dangerous and intensify the oedipally charged excitement of forbidden sexual behavior.

The structuring of sexual fantasies along direct and reverse triangulation may, paradoxically, intensify the passionate quality of love relations by the very reactivation of their oedipal significance and the endangerment of love by hatred. A broad spectrum of possibilities evolves from this point, ranging from highly satisfactory to devastatingly destructive. At one end of the spectrum, the uncertainty over the exclusiveness of love received from a spouse, the sense that life is an eternal struggle for reconfirmation of the stability, the intimacy, and the autonomy of the couple—its "territorial imperative," we might say, within the social group—increases love, gratitude, and mutual dedication. It is a powerful though largely unconscious bond cementing the couple. This double triangulation is typically expressed in sexual fantasies in which third parties are included during sexual play and intercourse. As I mentioned before, the fantasy of sexual involvement with another person, within an overall highly satisfactory sexual relation with a marital partner, is the most common secret of the sexual fantasy life of couples, a normal channel by which sexual stimulation and temptation from external sources can be redirected to the sexual life of the couple itself.

At the opposite extreme, the most destructive expression of direct and reverse triangulation is expressed in the chaotic invasion of the couple's love life by extramarital relations. Such relations maximize the revengeful implications of reversed triangulation, powerfully activate oedipal fears, traumatization, insecurity, and jealousy in both partners. Intense forms of jealousy, desperate efforts to destroy or devalue the marital partner who has become totally identified with the oedipal parental image, and the regressive activation of a full gamut of preoedipal conflicts all lead to a frequent form of chronic marital conflict.

Jealousy, vengeful rage, mourning over lost past idealizations, and (in simple terms), the loss of innocence, of the initial conscious expectations of the couple in love—these are a universal part of human reality. The experience of jealousy and betrayal, of the reconstitution of a good relation in the face of mutual aggression in it, are crucial actual or potential tasks for many couples, and under optimal circumstances may promote a deep understanding of the other person, as well as of one's own previously unacknowledged needs. This understanding may eventually result in the couple's having a very different level of relationship from their initial, conscious, mutual idealizations.

Once more, in discussing direct and reverse triangulation, we are faced with the central role of aggression in love relations, its exciting and activating function in tolerating the oedipal triumph, its destructive potential in the development of disruptive triangulations, jealousy, betrayal, revenge, and abandonment.

THE SUPEREGO AND THE EGO IDEAL:
ROMANTICISM AND CONVENTIONALITY

Freud defines the superego in "The Ego and the Id" as the unconscious internalization of parental oedipal prohibitions and parental demands that consolidate intrapsychically the prohibitions against incest and parricide, and signal the conclusion of the oedipal period of development. In recent psychoanalytic thinking this theory has also been subjected to significant modifications that are relevant for the psychology of sexual love and passion.[11] The internalization of the superego transforms external morality into an internal one, and that internal morality, it needs to be kept in mind, is subject to severe distortions because of projection and introjection. The recognition that these mechanisms transform objective commands and prohibitions from the parents into subjectively experienced ones has led to consideration of the contribution made by preoedipal conflicts to the nature of the postoedipal superego. Both Klein and Jacobson have pointed to the crucial importance of preoedipal determinants of superego functioning. The more severe the preoedipal conflicts, the more the superego is distorted by primitive fantasies, resulting in its fantastically prohibitive and demanding aspects.

Once more, the importance of aggression in the formation of intrapsychic structures is apparent. As a consequence of the consolidation of the superego, the child renounces the incestuous ties to the oedipal object and identifies himself or herself with the oedipal rival, postponing the gratification of oedipal wishes to the future. Under optimal circumstances, such identification and postponement strengthens the ego–ideal aspects of the superego; that is, it leads to a sense of morality and ethical values that provide gratification and stabilize self-esteem. An extremely aggressive superego may contribute to extending the prohibitions against incest to all subsequent sexual relations, and set up general demands for perfection that are impossible to achieve. This is the basic cause for the sexual inhibitions of individuals who have otherwise achieved the capacity for a differentiated and deep love relation.

In "Some Psychical Consequences of the Anatomical Distinction Between the Sexes" Freud proposed that, because castration anxiety and penis envy initiated the Oedipus complex in women, castration anxiety would not motivate the little girl to definitely renounce her oedipal object, thus leading to incomplete superego development in women; this idea has since been discarded by most psychoanalysts. In fact, Klein, Jacobson, Blum, and others convincingly point to the development of both normal and, in fact, often excessive structuralization of the superego in women as contrasted to men. The preoedipal contributions to women's superego derived from early maternal prohibitions and demands reinforce the oedipal prohibitions as well.[12]

Insofar as the superego has a general function of controlling aggression by activating unconscious guilt feelings and the derived capacity for conscious guilt, concern, and a sense of responsibility, the normal superego has a crucial role in protecting the couple against the activation of excessive aggression in sexual and generally intimate object relations that I referred to earlier. By the same token, the ego-ideal aspects of the superego evolve into setting up aspirations for the ideal love object (which reflects, in the last resort, the oedipal object) and thus reinforce oedipally derived longings with ethical aspirations and ideals that further contribute to individualize the love object.

Freud pointed out in "Group Psychology and the Analysis of the Ego" that, in the act of falling in love, the ego-ideal is projected onto the loved object and the libidinal investment of the ego-ideal is transferred onto the love object. This observation is of central relevance in the romantic aspect of falling in love that culminates during adolescence and is then maintained as an aspect of the romantic feature of love relations throughout life. Chasseguet-Smirgel in "Ego Ideal" has questioned the assumption that such a libidinal investment of a loved object "depletes" the libidinal investment of the self. She pointed out that, contrary to Freud's proposal, the love of an idealized object may increase the libidinal investment of the self as well by creating a relation in reality that replicates the ideal relation in fantasy between ego and ego-ideal. Under normal circumstances, falling in love increases self-esteem. The development of a severe decrease in self-esteem coupled with exaggerated idealization of a love object reflects the reactivation of oedipal insecurities and unconscious oedipal guilt.

The normal superego not only permits control of aggression, but also strengthens affectionate concern for the partner, consolidates a sense of moral responsibility for their mutual relationship, and protects the couple against the invasion of their boundary related to the consequences of direct and reverse triangulation. H. V. Dicks, in studying marital conflict, has suggested that what keeps couples together is, in addition to the gratification of their mutual sexual needs, the gratification of unconsciously activated object relations derived from oedipal and preoedipal levels of development.[13] These object relations are enacted by mutual projective identification, that is, the unconscious induction in the marital partner of a role that repeats, compensates for, or complements frustrating, feared, lost, or wished for relations from the past. In addition, Dicks proposed, a third factor that keeps couples together is the combined ideals of both partners regarding the kind of life they would like to lead together. Dicks described how such a combined or complementary integration of the couple's ego ideal, particularly in the context of a responsive cultural setting, may cement the relationship of a sexual couple even under conditions of external and intrapsychic conflict.

The principal negative influence of superego functioning of each partner on the couple's relationship, however, is the universal tendency for each partner to project unconscious superego features onto the other, so that rejected or repressed aspects of unconscious infantile morality re-emerge perceived as prohibitive attitudes in the partner. This development manifests itself most frequently in a subtle yet powerful tendency toward mutual sexual inhibition, perhaps the most frequent cause of sexual frustration, dissatisfaction, and boredom in otherwise harmonious sexual couples. A simple proof of this development is given by the surprising effects of sex therapy carried out with couples whose sexual functioning seems satisfactory to begin with. Most couples who have undergone sex therapy under such circumstances report a significant improvement in their sexual gratification and a resurgence of passionate love-making, which typically lasts for about six months. Sex therapists as symbolically parental authorities who "command" the enjoyment of sexuality may temporarily undo the cumulative effects of mutual superego projections.

Mature superego development in each of the partners may provide the couple with a sense of justice and proportion that may help to preserve its equilibrium. A realistic acknowledgment of one's own contribution to discord, to how one seduces the spouse into a situation leading into a triangular relation—an extramarital affair—the acknowledgment of the pain inflicted on the other person, and the paradox of happiness found in the forbidden affair matched by the implicit aggression against and betrayal of the partner who is also loved, may initiate benign cycles of mourning and reparative strivings and thus counterbalance the consequence of jealousy and envy. Normal guilt has potentially sublimatory functions.

The danger is that the sense of concern, a realistic sense of guilt and responsibility, derail into self-devaluation, an inability to tolerate one's own guilt, and into masochistic forms of expiation that directly feed into the sadomasochistic patterns of the couple. Or else, paradoxically, in defense against unbearable guilt, both partners may activate provocative behaviors with the unconscious expectation of severe punishment from the other, in the hope that such punishment will not coincide with total rejection by the partner.

The infantile nature of superego pressures operating on the couple, and exaggerated superego functioning, when mutually reinforced may result in an overdependence on socially sanctioned morality, and on conventional assumptions of "right" and "wrong" behavior, thereby intensifying guilt. Excessive guilt may take the form of denying normal reactions of jealousy and envy, as if such wishes were selfish or infantile.

At one extreme, then, severe superego pathology may deliver the couple to conventional values, morality, and expectations that may destroy their passionate relation. At the opposite extreme, insufficient development of superego functions may, in the short run, facilitate a degree of sexual freedom and the expression of polymorphous perverse sexual fantasies in highly gratifying sexual activities. In the long run, however, superego deficiency may result in breaking down the couple's boundaries, in the enactment of direct and reverse triangular relations, and, under extreme circumstances, in promiscuity culminating in group sex with its rapid deterioration of sexual excitement and boredom, paralleling the destruction of the couple's emotional bonds.

In contrast, the fantasy world of pornography may serve the useful function of activating in fantasy polymorphous perverse sexuality, which can be a source of sexual excitement and freedom for the couple, a rebellion against mutually induced infantile superego prohibitions, and a confirmation of a private world of sexual freedom that opposes social conventions without threatening the couple's integrity.

In this context it needs to be stressed, however, that erotic art provides an enactment of sexual fantasy within an aesthetic frame that represents a value system superimposed on the sexual activity and fantasy, a frame in turn related to the capacity for object relations in depth. In contrast, the conventionality—

and lack of an aesthetic frame—of pornographic material that presents purely mechanized sexual interactions has a strange but unavoidable self-defeating quality. The mechanical quality of vulgar pornography is, one might say, the counterpart of conventional supression of polymorphous perverse sexuality, both of them in contrast and opposition to the live erotic art of the secret, fantasied, and enacted sexual life of the couple.

Mass Psychology: The Couple and the Group

Freud in "Group Psychology" described the projection of the ego-ideal onto the leader of the horde, and the related mutual identification of all the followers in their idealization of the leader and identification with him. Under such conditions, the sense of individual responsibility disappears, an enormous sense of power permeates the group, and that sense of power combined with the freedom from moral constraints facilitates their following the leader in pursuit of destructive goals. In the postscript to this work Freud refers to the relation between the couple and the group. He suggests that two people coming together for the purpose of sexual satisfaction are demonstrating against the "herd instinct," the group feeling, and that the more deeply they are in love, the more is this true. Only when the affectionate part of a love relation yields entirely to the sensual one, he goes on, is it possible for two people to have sexual intercourse in the presence of others or for simultaneous sexual acts to take place in a group, as occurs in an orgy.

In *Internal World* I explored the relation between the couple and the group in the light of Freud's theory and other psychoanalytic studies of small and large group processes. In summary, I suggested that the couple in love represents both an ideal of and a threat to the large group, the fulfillment of each individual's fantasies. Each member of the group longs to break away from the anonymity of the large group and to become a partner in the private, secret, and symbolically forbidden new couple (the symbolic oedipal couple). At the same time, the group also experiences an intense envy of the couple that has managed to escape from the anonymous nature of the group, and to accomplish what each of the isolated individuals in the large group fear cannot be accomplished.

The wish to destroy the couple, derived from deep preoedipal sources of envy that tend to be activated under the conditions of large group processes and from direct oedipal rivalry and competition as well, resonates with the internal sources of aggression within the couple, referred to before—the ambivalence of their emotional relation, and the temptation to set up direct and reverse triangular relations. The couple needs the group to disperse in it the aggression that otherwise might destroy the couple in isolation. The triumph of the couple that maintains itself within the threatening conditions of the large group reinforces its bonds. Couples and large groups need each other and threaten each other, especially when groups are unstructured, such as in informal community meetings, political rallies, congresses, public celebrations and recreational events, and large informal parties. The couples' ordinary social life reduces the manifestations of these group processes, but maintains the tension between the boundaries of each couple and the threat to these boundaries derived from the activation of direct and reverse triangulation. In fact, the sexual tensions generated within the network of couples are a major cohesive force of social life as well as a threat to individual couples.

The relation to the leader of the horde, described by Freud, is transformed under ordinary social circumstances by the relation of a community to the common boundaries of conventional morality expressed in the laws regulating, among other issues, sexual relations. Such laws, as illustrated in the Judeo-Christian tradition in the Ten Commandments (and the expanded version of them in Leviticus 18, 19, and 20 of the Old Testament) are basically directed against incest and parricide, and geared to protecting the boundaries of sexes and generations against massive invasion by regressive polymorphous perverse sexuality under the dominance of primitive aggression. Chasseguet-Smirgel has detailed these functions of institutionalized morality in opposition to dangerous regression to primitive group processes that would tend to deny the prohibition against incest and parricide together with the exclusive nature of the oedipal couple and of the autonomous adult couple as its derivative. [14]

I would add that the collective projection of infantile superego features upon the abstract systems of laws and moral authority that regulate public behavior within informal human communities cannot but transform rational moral law into a derivative form of morality heavily influenced by infantile prohibitions against sexuality. This distortion takes the form of a conventionalized tolerance of sexuality that affirms the sacred nature of the autonomous couple, but suppresses the recognition of all elements of polymorphous perverse infantile sexuality, together with setting up a ritualization of sexual behavior that tends to reduce the private freedom of the couple.

These developments generate an unresolvable contradiction between public and private morality, a hidden contradiction between the couple's strivings for sexual freedom and the public restriction of sexuality to conventional social norms.

Paradoxically but not surprisingly, group rebellion against such conventional morality destroys both the conventional suppression of polymorphous perverse sexuality and the protection of the couple's sexual love. The protective functions of the superego are brushed aside together with its sexually restrictive ones. Group processes that illustrate this phenomenon are seen in boys' latency groups wherein sex is talked about freely but with derisory and largely anal terminology; in adolescent groups that, in the case of boys, also permit free communication about mechanical sexuality devoid of emotional value, and, in the case of girls, romanticize but degenitalize the idealization of popular stars.[15] Similar devaluation of the integration of erotic and tender love, and of the sexual passion of the couple, can be observed in the cultural atmosphere of "old boys' clubs" and their female equivalents. The experimental setting up of large, temporary, informal groups for the purpose of exploring large group behavior again illustrates how references to sexual issues rapidly deteriorate into aggressive and anally tinged comments, with couples tending to go underground under such circumstances.[16]

From a historical perspective, repeated cultural oscillations can be observed between "puritanical" periods in which love relations become de-eroticized and eroticism goes underground, and "libertine" periods in which free sensual sexuality deteriorates into emotionally degraded group sex. In my view, such oscillations reflect the long-term equilibrium between the dynamics of the social need for destroying, protecting, and controlling the couple, and the couple's aspirations to break out of conventional constrictions of sexual morality, a freedom that, *in extremes,* becomes self-destructive.

From this viewpoint, the so called sexual revolution of the 1960s and 1970s would reflect one more swing of the pendulum within conventional morality, and indicate no real change in the deeper dynamics of the relationship of the couple and the social group. Obviously, the broad spectrum of a couple's adaptation to conventional morality, from the conventionalism related to a lack of autonomous superego development, to the opposite conventionalism of submerging into large group processes is potentially present at all times, and the surface behavior of couples may vary enormously according to conventional pressures on a determinate social group. By the same token, the autonomous and mature sexual couple maintains its boundary of privacy in its capacity for secret passionate involvement under any but the most extreme social environments.

It is of interest that not only conventional moral wisdom but also conventional art tends to de-emphasize eroticism. "Kitsch" art, presenting reality in naive and pseudochildish ways, tends to portray human relations as devoid of ambivalence and complexity. Kitsch offers sentimentality rather than feelings. Its giving precedence to form over content is matched by pretentiousness and an obviousness that reinforces an atmosphere of childlike innocence and sexual purity. We also find the sentimentalization of traditional fairy tales, of romantic love in adolescence, of criminality as one aspect of human tragedy, the de-aggressified and de-eroticized triangulation of human conflicts as characteristics of mass media communication. Such erotic stimuli as are warranted by commercial advertisement provide a counterpart to depersonified eroticism, the complement of sentimental romanticism.

Conventional social norms that protect public morality are crucial in protecting the sexual life of the couple. The pressures for conventional behavior, however, are in contrast to the individual sophisticated value systems each couple has to establish for itself. The pressures for group formation along sexual lines, and for expression in such group formation of the primitive, shared mutual suspicion and hatred between men and women characteristic of latency and adolescent groups also threaten the couple.

If we compare the characteristics of conventional morality in present-day communist totalitarian societies, on the one hand, and contemporary Western societies, particularly this country, on the other, a curious paradox emerges. The restrictions on public discussion of and expression of sexuality in the Soviet Union, and China, for example, seem analagous to the sadistic suppression of sexuality carried out by the primitive superego of neurosis. At the same time, such sadistic superego control is effective in reducing random manifestations of individual violence in unstructured social situations.

In contrast, the predominant conventional ideology in our society is one of open discussion and expression of certain aspects of sexuality, with a simultaneous trend to mechanical engineering of sexual behavior, suppression of infantile polymorphous sexual components in culturally sanctioned mass entertainment, and open tolerance of violence, including sexual violence, in the same mass media. It is as if our conventional culture, rather than illustrating the pathology of a sadistic, though neurotic superego structure, illustrates borderline pathology with superego deterioration, regressive condensation of eroticism and aggression, and splitting of the erotic components of sexuality from their object-relations matrix.

It is as if today we were "privileged" to observe, in simultaneous action, relative extremes of the historically alternating pendulum movement between sexual puritanism and sexual libertinism, with both extremes revealing the flatness of all conventionally tolerable sexuality—in contrast to the potential richness of its private dimension in the individual couple. It is true, of course, that there is an enormous difference between a totalitarian regime's suppression of individual freedom that brutally imposes a conventional morality, and a democratic society's tolerance of a significant gap between conventionality and the private freedom of individuals and couples.

I think that there exists an irreducible dialectic between conventional morality and the private morality that each couple has to construct as part of its total sexual life, and that always implies a nonconventional degree of freedom the couple has to achieve for itself. The delicate balance of sexual freedom, emotional depth, and an integrated value system reflecting mature superego functioning is a complex human achievement that provides the basis for a relation that is deep, passionate, conflicted, while satisfying and potentially lasting. The integration of aggression and of polymorphous perverse infantile sexuality into a stable heterosexual relation are tasks for the individual and the couple. They cannot be achieved by social manipulation, but, fortunately, cannot be suppressed either, except under the most extreme circumstances by the conventions of society.

Two Cheers for Romance

STANLEY CAVELL

By the title of these remarks I mean to indicate both that
romance is of more value than is assigned it in the recent
assessments of it I have looked at, but also, of course, that it
is not worth a full-hearted three cheers. And at the same time
I was glad to hark back across decades to E. M. Forster's
Two Cheers for Democracy, remembering still its concrete, hu-
mane efforts—the likes of which seemed to me rare and valuable
even where I did not share its specific intuitions—to balance
(that is, to live) in our everyday returns of cares and obligations,
the claims of the best available manners and politics together
with the various claims of the most valued personal relationships. The way I speak of romantic marriage in the pages
that follow is meant at all times to register—if inadequately,
then as if for future reference—the out-turned public and the
in-turned private faces implicit in the concept of marriage;
faces that, could they but see one another, would betray one
another's secrets.

. . .

The brochure announcing the symposium for which the
present essay was composed contains a melancholy list of problems about love—conceptual problems tumbling on top of

biological and social issues—for which nothing in the way of solutions seem to be hoped for. And its text includes a pair of what it calls "historical facts" from which I would like to take some bearings in broaching what I have to say on this occasion. These facts are "the lack of a universal cultural identification between love and marriage and, in our own culture, the relatively recent preference, even yearning, for a marital relationship based on romantic love." A specification of this line of thought, and a claim arising from it, are to be found in a recent collection of essays entitled *Women: The Longest Revolution* by Juliet Mitchell, whose other writings include the influential *Psychoanalysis and Feminism*. In the section entitled "Romantic Love" she undertakes to "reformulate the whole conception of the shift in romantic love from medieval to modern times." I will quote from this chapter at some length both for its own interest and because I will be taking exception to some of its formulations.

Mitchell cites two feminist writers as precursors of her view. From Shulamith Firestone's *The Dialectic of Sex* she quotes these lines among others:

> As civilization advances and the biological bases of sex class crumble, male supremacy must shore itself up with artificial institutions. . . . where formerly women have been held openly in contempt, now they are elevated to states of mock worship. Romanticism is a cultural tool of male power to keep women from knowing their condition.

And the thesis of Germaine Greer's *The Female Eunuch,* summarized by Mitchell, joins the rise of Protestantism with

> a new ideology of marriage. . . . Marriage would no longer be an arranged business deal between powerful lineages. . . ; it had to be seemingly free and equal. Because of this, from having been the sort of fantasy province of a small nobility, romantic love came to replace parental coercion as that which forced one into marriage. From being excitingly adulterous and oppositional to the status quo in the Middle Ages, romantic love became a prelude to Establishment marriage of modern times.

Mitchell's own feminist account is that the new ideology of marriage, as a contract between equals, left equality merely "notional" (say, verbal) and that "romantic love shifted from being the male subject's search for his lost feminine self to being a consolation for a woman's future confinement in domesticity." Mitchell's more ambitious formulation takes into account what happens to the man as well as what happens to the woman in the shifting of romantic love. Beyond the feminist writers, she bases her own view also on Denis de Rougement's *Love in the Western World* (published in 1940), which she regards as "still the classical book on the subject of love." De Rougement proposes a more fundamental, less historically specific characterization of romantic love as something inherently in contradiction with marriage because inherently it is not about sexuality; it is opposed to the propagation of the species; it is, this romantic love, essentially about a mystical quest for union with lost regions of the self. Mitchell summarizes de Rougement's "central thesis" by saying: "What seems to go together is not love and marriage, but love and death." (You get a feel for de Rougement's perception here if you think of a region of works Mitchell does not mention, such as *Romeo and Juliet, Antony and Cleopatra, Tristan and Isolde, Emma Bovary, Anna Karenina.*) Mitchell counters de Rougement's refusal to translate what he describes as a religion of romantic love into sexual terms, and she goes on to interpret his descriptions of romantic love's narcissism and bisexualism as fitting what we understand as pre-Oedipal, pregenital sexuality. This allows her to ask us, surely sensibly, to realize that "if the women cannot be romantic lovers as subjects of their own search for self, men cannot be so either;" and that the "false sexual equality" in later romantic novels produces endings that, as they imagine "the confinement and the submission of the woman," usually find "some form of emasculation of the man."

All this seems to me worth pondering, but certain aspects trouble me from the start. Are these criticisms of marriage that is based on romance directed at what marriage of necessity has become under the pressure of romance, or are they directed at the changing historical forms romantic marriage has so far discovered for itself? Consider that government by consent (the modern liberal state) has arisen in the Western world within the period following the supposedly romantic shift. It too has bad things to answer for. And you can say, analogously, of government by consent that the consent is merely notional and that such government has become merely a consolation for the private citizen's future confinement to domesticity, or say to privacy; that is, to a life essentially without his or her own political voice. But in what spirit are such criticisms made? They are criticisms that democracy has made of itself, and which it forever tries to keep itself open to. But are we to take it that we know now of some better aspiration in favor of which the idea of government by consent is to be abandoned? Or are we—as I think—bound to be faithful to such government because only within it can truer consent be hoped for and achieved?

The critics of romantic marriage that I was citing, however, do not describe a form of marriage they could want, or give a sense of what good may be hoped for and achieved in marriage initiated by romance. They seem rather to concede fully that whatever good can be said of the institution has been said by its own ideologues; for example, by writers of popular romances, the sort of thing Henry Fonda, in Preston Sturges' film *The Lady Eve,* says he must sound like as he declares his eternal love to Barbara Stanwyck; he calls what he sounds like "a drugstore novel."

Juliet Mitchell takes her literary evidence for the views she gives of romance and marriage importantly from drugstore novels ("The popular romantic novels by Barbara Cartland or Denise Robbins, or stories in women's magazines"), and it is on this basis that she claims that "we no longer have a dominant strain of romantic literature in which the man is the subject of the passion." Essential as the evidence of drugstore literature may be, what causes this extraordinary reliance on its all-but-exclusive authority for what our culture tells itself about love and marriage? I propose to go on (in the space allotted me) to take the testimony of another dominant source of romantic fable that Mitchell has either forgotten about or has not experienced, that of the classical Hollywood film at its best. And I will introduce my discussion of two such films by noting the pertinence to our subject of a play of Shakespeare's, an item which can also be found in our finer drugstores.

If it can sensibly be claimed of any work central to our high culture that it represents, even schematizes, the shift from marriage as political (or social or economic) arrangement to marriage as romantic alliance, it can so be claimed of *Antony and Cleopatra*. Now if we go to that work for instruction about this shift, do we find that the woman is not the subject of her own story but merely its object, say its victim? This is what the men of the play may like to believe, and try to achieve, Octavius Caesar most consistently, whose fond desire is to keep Cleopatra from suicide so that he may trail her behind his triumphant chariot in Rome as his chief trophy. And are we prepared to say that Mark Antony forgoes his quest for his lost feminine self? There are indeed invitations at the end of his story to take him as emasculated. But what has caused this? I guess at least half of its readers would like to say, again with the Romans of the play, that Cleopatra is the cause, which more or less means that the cause is the conquering of marriage by romance. But there are major reasons also for denying that this is what Shakespeare's play takes the cause to be, from among which I pick two: (1) what Cleopatra wants from Antony is what she calls marriage, she wants him as in her word a husband; (2) Antony leaves Cleopatra in the first act on hearing that his wife Fulvia is dead, and returns to Cleopatra only when he is again safely and legally married at Rome. I do not know of any critic of this play who records this second pair of facts, but recording them helps me to propose as follows: the first half of the play gives a portrait of a man whose type Freud characterized in the famous sentence (from "The Tendency to Debasement in Love") "Where they love they do not desire and where they desire they cannot love;" but the play then takes this man to a state in which he is defeated not by the hopeless attempt to maintain this split but in the hopeful attempt to overcome it.

What I think of as the moral of the play is that no one any longer knows what marriage is, what constitutes this central, specific bond of union, as if it is up to each individual pair to invent this for themselves. Society can no longer ratify it, say after Luther denied that marriage is a sacrament and after Henry the Eighth showed that the political arrangements of marriage are themselves subject to the dictates of romance. Society is itself in need of ratification, perhaps by way of individuals consenting to it as a place within which to plight their troth. When, for example, Spencer Tracy harangues Katharine Hepburn in *Adam's Rib* (where they play a married pair of lawyers who take opposite sides in a courtroom case concerning a wife and mother of three who has shot her husband); harangues her, chastising her for forgetting that what marriage is, is a contract, as defined by the law; one feels that this is his anger speaking, that he is denying half of the truth, leaving out the heart of the matter.

I draw the moral of *Antony and Cleopatra* directly from the fact of its last act, which I interpret as the effort—on the part of Cleopatra and Shakespeare—to invent a new form of marriage ceremony, one in which the woman presents herself as a Queen, a mother, a nurse, an actress, and a lover, and in which the enormity of her narcissism and bisexuality is broken into by nothing less than a marriage with or in heaven itself. Among her dying words is the astoundingly daring cry, "Husband, I come", which transforms the idea of death that de Rougement associates with romance into an orgasm that mystically creates their marriage in eternity. I am not asking anyone— any more than I assume Shakespeare was—simply to adopt this as one's preferred wedding ceremony. But I do assume that the play's working asks us to consider what our fantasies are of the way in which, as in the classical formulation of marriage, two become one. That these fantasies may invoke the discharge of earth into heaven suggests that de Rougement's insistence on the dimension of the mystical in romance should not so hastily be reduced.

That no one any longer knows what creates the bond, the union, of marriage, is also the moral I have derived (in *Pursuits of Happiness*) in studying a group of the best Hollywood romantic comedies of the 1930s and 1940s, a group I name comedies of remarriage. It is from these and related movies that I would like now to suggest a working formulation of what I referred to a few minutes ago as an imagined new good of romantic marriage, of something that might suggest what hope there is in it, why certain versions of it (perhaps not those pictured in the "dominant strain of romantic literature" that Juliet Mitchell focuses on) might be worth struggling with from within. I assume that the new good to be hoped for from romantic marriage has something to do with the discovery of, or the need of, some new dimension of the *personal* in relations between the sexes, a mutuality not quite political and an intimacy not exclusively sexual. If I call it a new discovery of privacy, this may serve to align this quest with the risks of the new idea of government by consent. Marriage looked at from this perspective would be the name of some new way in which men and women require of one another that they bear the brunt of one another's subjectivity, in relative insulation from the larger world of politics and religion, which (for now at the least) has rejected this subjectivity, or let it loose.

Had I kept to an economy for these remarks that would have preserved my original title "Romanticism and Skepticism," my claims for a new imagination of, or pressure on, romantic marriage over the past few centuries would have been even more extreme. I would have interpreted the idea of bearing the brunt of one another's subjectivity as providing (or sustaining the) proof of one another's existence, and I would have gone on to argue as follows: When Descartes came upon modern philosophical skepticism in the seventeenth century (the problem of the human capacity to know anything at all, beginning with the existence of the world, the problem that produced his famous pivotal conclusion: "I think, therefore I am"), one of his goals was to establish that he was, as he puts it, not alone in the universe. To establish this, nothing less than a proof of God's existence (on the basis of the indubitability of that "I am") was required of his philosophical powers. As philosophy—say in Hume and in Kant—knew itself no longer possessed of such powers, major romantic writers (in America, Emerson and Thoreau, and Hawthorne and Poe, for example) proposed an idea of marriage, call it daily mutual devotedness, as the only path left us for walking away from exactly that skeptical doubt of cosmic isolation. In Emerson and Thoreau this devotedness is first of all due the universe itself, or say nature; to be faithful there one might have to leave what we mostly call marriage. One should feel that this shows a certain bravery of imagination in Emerson and Thoreau; but then one had better also consider the extent to which it shows their cowardice of imagination. In Hawthorne and in Poe, domesticity is more literally pictured as the marriage of human beings. The horror in their writings is accordingly a function of the idea that marriage cannot bear up under its metaphysical burden of ensuring the existence of one's other, hence of partaking of the other's securing of one's own existence. In one of Hawthorne's many tales of marriage ("Wakefield"), the narrator—I leave open the question of his tone—describes a man who has abandoned his marriage, for no comprehensible reason, as an "Outcast of the Universe."

In *Pursuits of Happiness,* the name I give to the new requirement upon romantic marriage, as reflected in the Hollywood comedy of remarriage, is the requirement of conversation. I take up the idea of conversation from John Milton's great tract on divorce (written roughly in the period in which Descartes was meditating his doubt and its overcoming), in which Milton defines marriage as "a meet and happy conversation" (and by "conversation" he does not mean just talk, but he does definitely also mean talk). Milton's tract, written as a theological defense of divorce, is at the same time a defense of the Puritan Revolution, and in claiming that sacred bonds may be dissolved when the meet and cheerful conversation for which they were entered into falls into a melancholy and intractable silence, it is clear that he is referring to the consent that creates legitimate government as much as to the agreement that constitutes marriage. (As if legitimacy altogether is now to be decided in the freedom of individual consciousness. No wonder marriage would be looked to as a way to share this terrible burden of individual authority. John Locke's more famous justification of consent, in his *Second Treatise of Government,* with its subdued description of the terrible cost of withdrawing consent—as it were of seeking to divorce society—was being written a dozen years after *Paradise Lost* appeared.)

The pair of films I will invoke here are from the era of the great remarriage comedies, but unlike those comedies they do not *show* us what a marriage may look and sound like that can bear the new exchange of subjectivity, the modern brunt of intimacy. They virtually do not *show* marriage at all (as if declaring our inability to recognize it any longer), and as if to emphasize this fact they contain a full complement of widows, widowers, bachelors, old maids, divorcées, and derelict or isolated husbands. I take them as showing, instead, how a newly conceived marriage may be pursued, or how, failing that possibility, marriage may rationally be rejected in favor of a life that promises something better than the old possibility.

The first of the pair is *Mr. Deeds Goes to Town* (directed by Frank Capra in 1936, starring Gary Cooper and Jean Arthur), one of the central so-called "screwball comedies"; and the second of the pair is a melodrama, or what used to be called a "woman's film"—*Now Voyager* (1942, starring Bette Davis, Paul Henried, and Claude Rains). Both films show the therapy of love in the form of the therapy of romance, of passion not as the goal of love but as the awakening of love, to the very possibility of accepting mutuality with another. I mean the phrase "therapy of love" in allusion especially to Freud's fullest piece of literary interpretation, lavished on Wilhelm Jensen's romantic fable *Gradiva*, in which the woman Gradiva's procedure in leading her rightful but perplexed lover to marriage with her is dwelt on by Freud to bring out its similarity to the procedure of psychoanalytic psychotherapy, viewed as what Freud there calls a love-cure. I regard these films as, at the very least, the artistic equal of Jensen's tale, fully worth the attention Freud gave the tale. And these are films of worldwide fame and popularity; in principle we could here have them in common, or three hundred others like them, at our disposal for our mutual instruction. I say "in principle" because of course I know that in fact we do not have them in common. And I do not just mean that some of you will not in fact have seen these particular films. Some of you will not have read, or may not well remember, *Antony and Cleopatra* either, but you will not think it odd for someone to speak of it seriously. (Perhaps you should.) I do not believe we know why it seems odd to discuss such films with the same seriousness. Given my conviction in the value of these films, I think one should find their popularity remarkable. Since commonly their popularity is taken as given, the claim that they are intellectually rich is commonly found to be incredible. Such is the uncreative position to which our culture so often in such cases confines itself.

In *Mr. Deeds Goes to Town*, a country boy who plays the tuba and composes popular verses for greeting cards (a reasonable emblem of popular movies) inherits $20 million from a remote uncle, goes to New York to collect, shows he is naturally smarter than the city slickers but not smart enough to overcome their political power. He is arrested on the complaint of his uncle's lawyers, who claim that his attempt to give away his fortune shows him to be mentally incompetent; at the same time he learns that the woman he has fallen in love with is a devious reporter who, using his feelings for her to extract a sensational series of newspaper features, has held his escapades up to ridicule, naming him "The Cinderella Man." At his sanity hearing he at first refuses to speak in his own defense, even against further testimony that he is, in the words of a comic expert Viennese psychiatrist, "obviously verruckt," and in the word of old maid sisters from his home town, "pixilated." After the woman reporter declares in open court that she loves the young man he successfully rises to his defense—not exactly by proving that he is not mad, but just that he is no madder than the common run of humanity—causes general social ecstasy, and wins the embraces of his beloved.

Mr. Deeds, like certain other romantic comedies, spends half of its energy ridiculing romantic love, the principal spokesperson of this ridicule being the principal woman of the plot who, of course, will eventually herself succumb to it. Her subjection to passion becomes a lesson in humility, in humanity you might call it, teaching her the defensiveness of her previous pride in her cleverness and autonomy. Since the man speaks several times about his wish to rescue a damsel in distress, you may join the woman in ridiculing his fantasy of marriage as a fairy tale romance, and then go beyond this by ridiculing the woman in turn for succumbing to this fantasy. And you may cap your superiority to the film by repeating the most frequent view of such movies that finds its way into words— namely, that they are fairy tales for the depression, made to help distract the populace from its economic misery. In this view such movies ask little more of us, in addition to a willingness to be pleased (no small matter), than to believe that their ending may be formulated in words such as, "They lived happily ever after." What we are shown in *Mr. Deeds*, for example, is something I find to be distinctly different. The woman can be said to *become* a damsel in distress, but just in a sense in which the man can equally be said to have discovered himself as another damsel in distress. Distress turns out on this showing to be the access and confession of desire. The mutuality of desire confuses and frightens the pair, for all their separate, shrewd strengths, but they at last commit themselves to pursue it together. In the closing image of the film the man lifts the woman in the middle of a now mostly empty courtroom, as if to carry her over a threshold, and they stand there kissing repeatedly as the music swells. (I guess not just the music.) Of course you can say that this is Hollywood code for their living happily ever after. But you can alternatively appropriate this image in terms that to my mind it more accurately invites, interpret it to say that no one, including the pair, knows how to arrive at the threshold to which they are drawn, that the threshold is of some inner place they have to discover together, and that marriage is the name of this adventure or quest that they are committing themselves to, with no assurance of success.

In Deeds' defeat of the Viennese psychiatrist (one of his feats of overcoming that elicits the world's acceptance of him and the woman's consent to love for him), we again have before us a choice of interpretations. You may take Deeds' victory over the foreign thinker to be a sign of Capra's American anti-intellectualism; or you may take it, as I do, that we are shown a contest between approaches to psychological understanding, and that Deeds' victory is of psychological awareness—or aliveness in principle open to ordinary human beings, and inevitably open to those who are open to it—over certain claims to a privileged expertise that is closed to that openness.

Now Voyager also features a psychiatrist, but as in other Hollywood melodramas—as opposed to its comedies (a matter for critical speculation)—the role is positive and it is instrumental in achieving the therapeutic success of the film. I must sketch this film a little less briefly.

The good psychiatrist, Dr. Jaquith (Claude Rains), tells the tyrannical mother of Charlotte Vale (Bette Davis) that Charlotte is having a nervous breakdown and he recommends residential therapy at his clinic in the country, called Cascades. Residence at Cascades produces in Charlotte the most dramatic metamorphosis that I know of in film, as she goes from aggressive plainness to dazzling attractiveness. (A sub-text of the movie is given when Charlotte's mother refers to her as "my ugly duckling.") Charlotte, transformed, is sent on a cruise to try out her new wings, and that is where she meets Jerry (Paul Henried), travelling alone because his wife is too sickly to share any fun. Jerry is worried about his daughter Tina, whom Charlotte at once divines was not wanted by the wife. Henried performs his world-historical romantic trick of lighting two cigarettes at the same time and then handing one to Bette Davis. What I am calling the therapy of romance in this film is epitomized by an inspired sequence in which, while the two of them are at dinner on shipboard, Charlotte is overcome by what strikes her as the fraudulence of her situation. She shows Jerry a family photograph of the Boston Vales, about which he asks: "Who is the funny fat lady with all the hair?", and the now slender, impeccably dressed and groomed, ravishing Bette Davis replies, "I am the funny fat lady with all the hair." One feels that this extraordinary revelation of her inner identity is meant to defend herself from further facing her desire, released toward this dashing yet kind stranger; at the same time the strength to make the revelation is essentially a function of the very metamorphosis of desire which he has helped to establish. He is not put off by the dark side of the fantasy of the ugly duckling (namely, what it was from which metamorphosis was called for, hence the stain of doubt that the metamorphosis really happened); and accepts her identity in her suffering while at the same time accepting her identity as she is. She knows that she will be grateful to him for this forever. Her return to Boston is a sequence of triumphs—over her mother, over her wider family, over her social circle. She attracts the love of a handsome, socially perfect widower her mother is desperate for her to marry, but she breaks her engagement to him in the knowledge that her life remains elsewhere. (So it is not true of Charlotte that she is coerced into marriage either by a formidable parental wish for alliance of family fortunes or by the promise of romance.) On returning for respite to Cascades she encounters Jerry's daughter Tina who has become a patient there and with whom she forms a therapeutic alliance, something none of the professional staff has been able to do. Charlotte thus becomes the good mother to her lover's child as well as to herself. After her own mother's death she transforms the mausoleum of the Vale mansion into a life-enhancing haven for young and old, recognizes that Jerry is stuck in his guilty marriage, convinces him and Dr. Jaquith to let her continue to mother Tina, and devotes her fortune to expanding Cascades, where Dr. Jaquith appoints her to the board of directors.

I give this somewhat mocking summary of the film (it is of critical interest that summary inherently tends toward mockery), which I hope at the same time suggests my great admiration for it, in order to go on to pose a question which we cannot answer in the absence of the film itself. Granted that some asymmetry is proposed between this man and this woman (that is, equality and reciprocity between them is ruled impossible) in whose favor is the asymmetry cast? I gather that a certain feminist reading of such a film would run as follows: Marriage under those social conditions, as under present conditions, would have been confining enough, but this hopeless romance, this prohibition of marriage, is even worse. Here the woman is relegated to child-rearing and house-managing and man-serving with no compensating social role whatever and with no real private—that is, erotic—compensation either. Her value is assessed as merely a function of social nobleness earned through self-sacrifice. This view is obviously consistent with the various ideologies of marriage cited and extended by the accounts of Juliet Mitchell, to the effect that women have to be made to want marriage (as still conceived).

The trouble with this view of the film is that it is essentially Jerry's view of what Charlotte is doing. It is he who says to her: "No self-respecting man would allow such self-sacrifice as yours to go on indefinitely." And I find that my response to this sentiment is well represented by Charlotte's response to Jerry's statement: "That's the most conventional, pretentious, pious speech I ever heard in my life." And when a moment later he tells her: "You should be trying to find some man who'll make you happy," her reply is withering (and remember that it is Bette Davis saying the words, slowly, as if seeking to fathom the origin of each of them): "Some man who'll make me happy? I've been laboring under the delusion that you and I were so in sympathy, so one, that you'd know without being asked what would make me happy." This turns out to be something she describes as their sharing a "fancy" of making a place for his unwanted child to achieve metamorphosis. After a few more words, and with a last pair of cigarettes lit, Jerry asks: "And will you be happy, Charlotte?", to which Charlotte replies with the famous closing lines of this film: "Oh Jerry, let's not ask for the moon; we have the stars."

Granted that you can appropriate this ending in Jerry's guilty way, I close by sketching another way of appropriating it. Charlotte's closing speeches are about the two of them "being one," which I noted as our classical conceit for being married. She says in effect that the condition of this state is the sharing of fantasy, which she believed was satisfied in their case; which is to say, she took them to be in a state of marriage. Doubtless it is not all a marriage might be, but what marriage is? How much it may be is recorded in her saying to the man, "We have the stars." I take this to imply that they have had a share of the moon, it is in place, the metamorphosis was achieved. If we now take the image of stars against the image from Hawthorne about finding oneself an Outcast of the Universe when we abandon the thing we are rightfully wedded to, she is saying: We are not such outcasts, that much salvation is ours. I think it is clear that Jerry does not get the idea and that he is, and so to speak prefers being, cast out, wedded to that remove. Charlotte's discovery that she and Jerry are not, as it were, married is evidently harder for her to bear than her earlier discovery that something is more important to her than bed with Jerry. In both discoveries Charlotte has—forever with Jerry's help—quite transcended his orbit of comprehension. Accordingly, I cannot doubt that this is a romantic quest whose subject is the woman, with the principal man of the romance a self-appointed object or victim.

Now, finally, I will suggest that one possibility of constituting marriage is presented by this film as something more mysterious yet, in a way that the readers of this volume should find suspicious, but one that I hope we could in principle leave open. Jerry was brought to Charlotte's house, for that final interview with her, by Dr. Jaquith. (We will hear from Charlotte that the interview is Dr. Jaquith's test of Charlotte and Jerry's resolve not to pursue their private romance; to have the child together they must not do together what causes children. This still leaves open a question: is Dr. Jaquith's "test" meant to see whether the couple is capable of obeying his prohibition, or is it to provide Charlotte with an occasion for seeing that her economy of desire has shifted? Or rather her economies—she is involved in more than one household.) Before that interview we are given a moment in which Dr.

Jaquith and Charlotte are seated together òn the floor of her remodelled (metamorphosed) drawing room studying the architectural plans for the addition she is proposing for Cascades, the habitation they share. This image, colored by the feeling of the moment, I read as registering that these two are also married. Now before you jump to the conclusion that she has not resolved her transference in her relation with her therapist—a matter surely to be considered—I hope you will be willing to think of these words and images in terms of Freud's 1915 essay, "Observations on Transference-Love," in which he insists in all honesty on the point that "the state of being in love which makes its appearance in the course of analytic treatment (ie., the transference-love) has the characteristics of a 'genuine' love." The analyst does not act to fulfill this love in its own terms because it is exactly his or her peculiar task *not* to act on it, but instead to teach an attitude that allows freedom from the dictation of action by desire. One might say that it is only *because* transference-love is a version of real love that this learning can take place. The question for me is whether Charlotte Vale's modification and satisfaction of the various strands of her desire (and of the concept of marriage) may be imagined as achieving a credible and creditable degree of psychic freedom. She had written to Dr. Jaquith to inform him of breaking her engagement to the eligible widower, expressing her confusion over her action. This man, she said, offered everything a woman is supposed to want: a man of her own, a home of her own, a child of her own. Now in these terms my question about this film becomes: Do we see at its conclusion the life of a woman who has found the way to her version of these things, including work of her own? Or do we feel, on the contrary, that she has merely fallen into the grip of an ideology which forces her to find substitute compensations for the actual or literal possession of such things, as those things are themselves now only substitute compensations for the genuine autonomous quest for a woman's own existence?

We cannot sensibly begin now to respond to these issues, by screening the film and working through our experience of it together. That is a pity, but just a contingent fact. What is a thousand pities is something I noted earlier: that we do not ask such questions of such films even when the occasion for the asking might present itself, that is, even when we possess the film in common. And that is not just a contingent fact but a systematic work of self-deprivation. Our participation in this deprivation is eased by a pair of assumptions, one about the culture at large, one about its major films: according to the one assumption, our culture's romantic ideology of marriage, serving to depress a woman's quest for her own existence, goes essentially unchallenged by the culture at large; according to the other assumption, Hollywood movies are popular commodities whose possibilities are unproblematic and which, in particular, simply serve to support that ideology of marriage, since certainly they would not themselves help to challenge it. Both feminists and anti-feminists seem to have conflicting uses for this pair of assumptions. And the fear must be massive that keeps us unaware that movies at their best powerfully reflect back the culture's knowledge to itself of its own doubts and ambivalences concerning these very assumptions. Had I time to say why I initially put the idea of skepticism into the title of these remarks—the idea that are privately doubt that the world exists and ourselves and others in it—I might guess that the fear such movies divine in us is the fear of daily, repetitive, ordinary, domestic existence; the fear of finding it *and* the fear of not finding it, "it" being what you might call the marriage of romance with marriage.

The Riddle of Femininity and the Psychology of Love

CAROL GILLIGAN and EVE STERN

In the opening scene of *Love's Labour's Lost,* the King of Navarre turns his court into an Academe where he and his friends vow to live and study for three years without seeing women. In this way, he believes, they will come to know that "which else we should not know. . . . Things hid and barr'd from common sense."[1] Berowne, a courtier and one of the friends, protests that such truths may be blinding. Instead he suggests that enlightenment can be gained through common sense by looking in women's eyes:

> Study me how to please the eye indeed,
> By fixing it upon a fairer eye,
> Who dazzling so, that eye shall be his heed,
> And give him light that it was blinded by.[2]

The idea that knowledge can be gained from common sense and women's perceptions turns out, however, to require elaborate demonstration. Even when the King and his friends realize that they do not know the people they claim to love, they do not see why their project of love must fail. Yet in this

101

play that breaks romantic conventions—Jack hath not Jill; all is not well—love means relationship, rather than a self-enclosed passion. Thus self-knowledge must be joined to knowledge of the other. Socrates' dictum to "know thyself" is inadequate as a prescription for living in the world, and the lovers are sent off to discover how the other becomes accessible and known.

Shakespeare addresses this question of knowledge through the theme of language and illustrates the ways in which language reveals ignorance and can serve as a means for discovering truth. Rosaline, the wittiest of the women, underscores the relational dimensions of language when she observes that:

A jest's prosperity lies in the ear
Of him that hears it, never in the tongue
Of him that makes it.[3]

When the lovers have been fooled by the ladies' disguises to woo "but the signs of she,"[4] Berowne—her counterpart—forswears affectation and seeks to speak in "honest, plain words:"[5]

Henceforth my wooing mind shall be express'd
In russet yeas, and honest kersey noes.[6]

Yet for Berowne above all, it is only after the women continue to reveal what he is not seeing that he discovers how deeply entrenched are the problems in his way of speaking; he then undertakes, reluctantly, the task of accommodating speech to the facts and to the emotional realities of the listener as well as of himself.

The difficulty of knowing what in the end seems most simple and the reluctance to change a language that is demonstrably self-enclosed are the insights of psychoanalysis as well. The analytic situation dramatizes problems in seeing and speaking that lead love's labor to be lost, and it reveals the knowledge that must be gained if love is eventually to be won. The absence of a plain language of love in psychoanalytic writing is therefore surprising and raises the question of why simple words do not serve the psychologist's ends. The current replacement of "honest, plain words" like love, sorrow, joy, envy, and pain with the sterile terminology of object relations, where "mirroring relationships" and "holding environments" are intended to reflect and contain human passion, where lovers and mothers are renamed "significant others" and "attachment figures," reveals a language of love so strikingly devoid of people and feelings that it leads one to ask: what people and what feelings are being concealed?

If the technical vocabulary is traced back to its initial appearance, Freud introduces the terms "object" and "aim" in his "Three Essays on the Theory of Sexuality," where he also makes the statement that the "erotic life [of men] alone has become accessible to research. That of women is veiled . . . in an impenetrable obscurity."[7] Like the King of Navarre, psychologists have proceeded on the assumption that women are a source of distraction and confusion and can be excluded from consideration. To speak about love and sexuality while saying that one does not know about women implies that women's experience can be separated from human experience. To refer to people as "objects" and thus without subjectivity and perspective suggests that the story of love can be told from only one angle. Thus love and sexuality are divorced from relationships with people. As Freud modeled his concept of Eros on that "of the divine Plato," Socrates' dictum (to know thyself) remains the psychoanalytic prescription for love.

In drawing attention to the language of love within contemporary psychology and focusing on the gaps in the information provided, we wish to show how this change in language loses a story of love that is told commonly in simple terms. The central problem we address is the problem of objectification, as it impedes development and as it leads to a description of love independent of people and perspectives. The key to solving this problem is the premise that women's experience must be considered in *defining* human nature. Thus, rather than looking *at* women and asking how women exemplify current conceptions of love, we will look *through* the eyes of women and ask what light this perspective casts on the general understanding of love. In making woman the subject (the perceiver) rather than the object (the perceived) in the story of love, we will show how this shift in the angle of vision solves the riddle of femininity that has puzzled psychologists, and transforms the psychology of love.

. . .

Our interest in stories about love was spurred by reading the works of moral philosophers and psychoanalysts who are women. We looked at these writings to see how women resolved the tension inherent in their decision to work within a tradition that excluded their experience. We found the lost story of their experience represented by gaps in the writing, sudden contradictions, and inconsistencies in style that appeared when these women exemplified love and then sought to align their examples with the discipline within which they were writing. In novels written by women, we found descriptions of a search to recover a lost story of love. It was also our impression from interviewing adolescent girls that they often are tempted to become a mystery, to render themselves unknown, especially in their relations with boys. Like the women writers, the girls seemed willing to suspend disbelief in accepting traditional stories about love that were at odds with what they knew about relationships from their own experience. In the process, their own stories began to seem incoherent and then to disappear.

In order to recover a story about love that seems at once familiar and forgotten we rely on a work of literature because art admits a variety of perspectives and interpretations. Unlike psychology, literature is not burdened by the claim to an "objective frame." By reaching out of psychology and into literature with an eye to common sense and plain language, we aim to loosen the soil that has buried the story of women's experience, removing the thatch of a mystifying language in order to see what grows.

Thus we return to one of the oldest stories about passionate attachment, the myth of Eros and Psyche, or Cupid and Psyche in Apuleius' rendition, recorded in the second century A.D. To illustrate what happens to the story of love when one looks for the plain language and follows common sense, we introduce the story in its familiar reading, relying on Bruno Bettelheim's excellent synopsis:

> In this story, a king has three daughters. Psyche, the youngest, is of such extraordinary beauty that she arouses Aphrodite's jealousy, so Aphrodite orders her son Eros to punish Psyche by making her fall in love with the most abominable of men. Psyche's parents, worried because she has not yet found a husband, consult the oracle of Apollo. The oracle says that Psyche must be set out on

a high cliff to become the prey of a snakelike monster. Since this is tantamount to death, she is led to the assigned place in a funeral procession, ready to die. But a soft wind deposits her in an empty palace where all her wishes are fulfilled. There Eros, going against his mother's orders, keeps Psyche hidden away as his beloved. In the darkness of the night, in the disguise of a mysterious being, Eros joins Psyche in bed as her husband.

Despite all the comfort Psyche enjoys, she feels lonely during the day; moved by her entreaties, Eros arranges for her jealous sisters to visit Psyche. Out of their vile envy, the sisters persuade her that what she cohabits with and is pregnant by is "a huge serpent with a thousand coils," which, after all, is what the oracle seemed to predict. The sisters talk Psyche into cutting off the monster's head with a knife. Persuaded by them, against his orders never to try to see him, while Eros is asleep Psyche takes an oil lamp and a knife, planning to kill the beast. As light falls on Eros, Psyche discovers that he is a most beautiful youth. In her turmoil, Psyche's hand shakes, and a drop of hot oil scalds Eros; he awakes and departs. Heartbroken, Psyche tries to commit suicide, but is saved. Pursued by Aphrodite's anger and jealousy, Psyche has to suffer a series of terrible ordeals, including a descent into the underworld. . . . Finally, Eros, his wound healed, touched by Psyche's repentance, persuades Zeus to confer immortality upon her. They get married on Olympus, and the child born to them is Pleasure.[8]

This myth has been widely recognized by psychologists and feminists as a story not only about love but also about female development. In these interpretations, Eros and Psyche take on the status of abstraction, becoming for Erich Neumann the archetypal representation of the eternal masculine and feminine; for Bruno Bettelheim, the prototype for characters in animal-groom fairy tales; for Lee Edwards, Psyche becomes the model for modern superwomen.[9] In Bettelheim's view of female development, love depends on overcoming sexual disgust and claiming equality;[10] for Edwards it depends on claiming consciousness and exercising power;[11] for Neumann it hinges on conflict and separation followed by surrender and mystical transcendence.[12] In all of these views, development is contingent on an act of separation through which Psyche is transformed from a physical to a spiritual condition; her metamorphosis is from woman to soul.

In approaching Psyche simply as a person, rather than as a

mythic representation, a hero, or a symbol, we rely on the authority of her own words and actions, letting her and common sense guide our reading. We find that her story emerges when we approach her as a subject in the text, and the key to her story is her struggle against objectification. As this struggle emerges, the myth becomes a cautionary tale about interpretation; the reader who joins the people in the story by "marvel-[ling] at her divine beauty, but only as it were at some image, well-painted and set out,"[13] loses sight of Psyche as an interpreter.

Psyche herself warns against misreading her story in this way. When her parents prepare to take her to the high hill to die, they weep and grieve over her sad fate. Yet Psyche tells them that they are weeping for her at the wrong time:

> When the people did honour me with divine honours and all together call me new Venus, then you should have grieved, then you should have wept, then you should have sorrowed, *as though I had been then dead.*[14] (Italics ours.)

At the outset of the story, Psyche herself thus establishes the connection between objectification and death. Common sense affirms her perception: to be renamed a goddess is to lose one's own name. To become the personification of beauty is to lose one's life. It is understandable, then, why Psyche sets out "with strong gait"[15] to lead the procession to the high hill; rather than lamenting her funeral marriage, she welcomes this end to a life in which it was "as though [she] had been then dead."

Throughout the myth, death functions as a leitmotiv for objectification; each time Psyche is treated by others as an object, she moves toward killing herself. Objectification imperils Psyche's ability to exist as a person not only by denying her subjectivity and perspective but also by separating her from connection with others and thus from love. Isolation inevitably accompanies objectification—separation does not mean development here but loneliness that is tantamount to death.

This difference in interpretation is underscored by the failure of the oracle's prophecy. According to the oracle of Apollo, Psyche's sacrifice is a horrible fate; if we listen to Psyche, the terrible fate is the beauty of her adolescence which turns her into an object of worship and thus distances her from others and from herself:

> Psyche sitting at home alone lamented her solitary life, and being disquieted both in mind and body (although she pleased all the world) yet hated she in herself her own beauty.[16]

Following the funeral procession, Psyche is in fact not devoured by a monster; instead the funeral marriage signifies the death of "new Venus" as isolated object and prepares for the birth of Psyche through the experience of connection or love.

When Psyche is left alone on the hill, an extraordinary passage begins, capturing in a series of natural images the rhythms and sequence of female sexual awakening:

> There came a gentle air of softly breathing Zephyrus and carried her from the high hill, with a meek wind, which retained her garments up, and by little and little brought her down into a deep valley, where she was laid in a soft, grassy bed of most sweet and fragrant flowers.[17]

The story continues as Psyche awakens and enters a house of great beauty where her unknown husband visits her by night. "And so (as it naturally happened) that which was first a novelty, by continual custom did at last bring her great pleasure."[18]

This remarkably explicit description of female sexual experience, told as a story of nature, is followed by the story of a marriage conducted in darkness and a life of riches lived in the presence of disembodied voices that minister to her needs. Having come into a new connection with herself through the experience of pleasure, Psyche resumes her struggle against objectification in attempting to establish the nature of her connection to others. Thus a conflict arises between the sweetness of Eros' embraces and the harshness of his demands that she live

> closed within the walls of a fine prison, deprived of human conversation, and forbidden to aid or assist her sorrowful sisters, no, nor once to see them.[19]

The apparent hopelessness of Psyche's struggle against isolation and mystification leads her to despair: "she passed all the day in weeping and went to bed at night without any refection of meat or bathing."[20] As this neglect of her physical needs signals the return of objectification—the denial of her human nature, her need to see and speak to those she loves is established as a vital human need.

Psyche's pregnancy marks the turning point in this story about connection, since it gives her access to knowledge about herself and about her relations with others. Although it is Eros who announces the pregnancy to her, her own body gives her the evidence to gauge for herself: "she counted the days as they increased and the months that passed by, and marveled as the promise grew."[21] The child not only attests to her experience of connection gained through pleasure but it also embodies her connection with her mysterious husband whose "shape and face I shall learn at length by the child in my belly."[22] As the natural event of pregnancy becomes central to Psyche's quest for knowledge, it also moves her to take action to protect herself and her child.

Eros tells Psyche that if she keeps their relationship secret, she will bear an immortal god rather than a mortal child. Her sisters tell her that she lives with a monster who, at the time of delivery, will devour her and the child. Caught between conflicting stories and faced with a problem of interpretation, Psyche also has access to her own knowledge through her experience of connection with the child. "In diverse and doubtful opinions" and "stirred by so many furies,"[23] she chooses in the end to act on this knowledge and risk the immortal child she was promised in order to save the real child in her belly. Thus she takes a lamp and a razor, preparing to kill the monster. Yet looking at Eros under the light, she discovers him to be a most beautiful young man.

In violating the prohibition against seeing Eros, Psyche discovers that the stories she was told about her husband—by the oracle, by her parents, and by her sisters—were in fact not true. Instead, the knowledge of him that she gained through her own experience is confirmed by what she sees. Affirming herself as a perceiver and knower, Psyche positions herself firmly as a subject rather than an object in this story about love. This change in position is announced simply and clearly in the text: "and thereby *of her own accord,* she fell in love with Love."[24] (Italics ours.)

This striking statement calls into question the association of love with blindness and silence—the conditions Eros had imposed. But Psyche's act of perception, rather than destroying, instead transforms this story of love. To talk about love between two subjects, rather than between subject and object, means to talk about a relationship between two people—each capable of knowledge and sight. Yet Eros and Psyche as two knowers must gain access to each other's stories, and this access is gained through a series of trials. Although the trials would seem to be trials of separation, they are designed to reveal dependence as the condition of relationship and therefore of love.

Psyche, having discovered that the stories she was told by others are untrue, must learn that others can sometimes be trusted and that their knowledge may be true. Choosing love, she faces the seemingly impossible tasks that Venus has set and must rely on the ants, the sheep, the reeds, and the eagle who offer to show her the means to save her life. Each time, she initially attempts death, now in response to separation, but the world of nature intervenes to save her, reminding her of her human nature—that she is a creature of the land and not the sea—and also taking pity on her, seeing that she is "greatly in love."[25] These lessons in dependence lead in the end to a final confrontation with death—a day's worth of beauty in a jar. Now tempted, in her separation, by the allure of female objectification, Psyche yields to the danger in an effort "to please [her] lover" and once again is almost killed by beauty.[26] Once again she is rescued by Eros who, like Psyche, chooses love.

If Psyche's story about the dangers of objectification and separation has eluded past readers, Eros' story about connection is even more abstruse. His action in rescuing Psyche has been consistently misinterpreted as a response to her need. Neumann sees Eros respond to Psyche's voluntary willingness to sacrifice her whole being for him;[27] Bettelheim describes Eros as "touched by Psyche's repentance;"[28] Edwards, in an odd reversal, sees Eros as "rescued by Psyche when she makes him rescue her from Persephone's spell."[29] Yet the text in its plain language tells a simpler version:

Cupid being now healed of his wound and malady, [was] not able to endure the long absence of Psyche.[30]

Eros undergoes his own trial of separation that reveals to him his dependence, and his action is self-initiated in response to his consciously perceived need for Psyche. The absence he intended as punishment for her turns out to be punishing for him as well. Seen in this light, the physical wound he suffers from the oil of the lamp reveals a deeper psychic wound—manifest in his belief that his need for Psyche must not be spoken of or seen.

While Eros is ill, love is sick:

> there is now nothing any more gracious, nothing pleasant, nothing gentle, but all is become uncivil, monstrous, and horrible; moreover, there are no more loving marriages, nor friendships of amity, nor loving of children, but all is disorderly and there is a very bitter hatred of weddings as base things.[31]

His act of separation, undertaken in response to what he perceived as Psyche's betrayal ("O simple Psyche, consider with thyself, how I . . . did come myself from heaven to love thee"),[32] thus disrupts the order of love. When Eros recovers from his wound, his perception of Psyche changes. Taking "his flight towards his loving wife," he wipes the deadly sleep from her face; recognizing her "overmuch curiosity," he knows and loves her "more and more."[33]

Psyche, reminded again of the dangers of objectification, discovers that love can be trusted; once again the story she was told about love turns out not to be true. Her act of perception, violating Eros' prohibition, leads in the end to a "just" and "lawful" and "everlasting" marriage. As the lovers through their own actions gain access to knowledge of one another, Psyche becomes immortal and Eros becomes the father of a daughter named Pleasure.

The symbolism of the oil in this ancient story—not a cutting weapon but a source of light[34]—reveals problems in love to be problems of knowledge. As Psyche emerges from objectification to enter the story as both lover and mother, Eros's connection to her must be seen. The same darkness and silence that impeded Psyche's efforts to interpret her experience of connection also concealed from Eros the nature of his feelings for her. Told simply, this myth speaks directly to many modern mysteries, including the mystery of female sexuality, the mystery of female development, and the mystery of how love can be sustained through conflict and strife; thus the question arises: how did this story get lost to modern psychology?

. . .

Bruno Bettelheim, commenting on Freud's use of the Greek words "Eros" and "erotic," notes that for readers like Freud, who are steeped in the classical tradition, the word calls up not only Eros's charm and cunning but also "his deep love for Psyche, the soul, to whom Eros is wedded in everlasting love and devotion."[35] The word "psychoanalysis" which Freud coined thus carries with it, in Bettelheim's description, the double connotation of " 'Psyche' the soul—a term full of the richest meaning, endowed with emotion, comprehensively human and unscientific [and] 'analysis' [which] implies a taking apart, a scientific examination."[36] Bettelheim points out in *Freud and Man's Soul* that when the word "soul" becomes translated as "mind" in the Standard Edition of Freud's writings, psychoanalysis loses its emotional resonance and thus its quintessential meaning—the joining of the tools of reason to the substance of human feelings.[37]

But there is a deeper point to be made. The word "psyche" not only means soul but also refers to Psyche, the woman—and specifically the woman in love. The term psychoanalysis which Freud introduced in 1896 conveys the essence of his early work—the analysis of hysteria as a disorder of love in women. Thus psychoanalysis at the beginning was linked both with love and with women, and the change in psychoanalytic thinking which Bettelheim describes—the loss of emotional resonance and human connection—extends beyond the problems of translation to the replacement of Psyche with the word "object"—which appears in conjunction with Eros in 1905.

The *Three Essays on the Theory of Sexuality* which witness this conjugation also mark the beginning of the images of blindness and mystery which surround Freud's discussion of women—his statement that the sexual life of women is veiled in obscurity, his designation of the sexual life of adult women as "a dark continent for psychology,"[38] and his conclusion in 1933 that "the riddle of femininity" remains unsolved.[39] As Eros is joined to "object," Pleasure becomes an "aim" or later a "principle;" thus with the advent of a technical language for talking about sexuality and love, the female characters in the classical story become inhuman abstractions and disappear. Yet the sense of a lost story about love hangs around Freud's later writings as he puzzles over the mystery of female sexuality and the different path of female development.

Freud refers briefly to Psyche in his essay on "The Theme of the Three Caskets," published in 1913, so clearly her story was known. Her disappearance between 1896 and 1905, marked by a change in language that shifts the emphasis from "Psyche" to "analysis," may be explained by Freud's choice of the Oedipus story as *the* story of passionate attachment—a choice made in *The Interpretation of Dreams* which was written during this time. This is a story where love is connected to blindness rather than seeing, where passionate attachment ends in tragedy and death, the story summed up in Freud's statement that "the finding of an object is in fact a refinding of it,"[40] and a story that renders female development essentially incoherent. In all these respects, it differs from the Eros and Psyche myth.

Although the Oedipus story is interpreted as a tragedy of passionate attachment, this drama of love and blindness has its origins in an act of abandonment and separation. The act is carried out by Jocasta in an effort to save her husband from the child. Thus she makes the opposite choice from the one that Psyche makes. Both women set out to enact a division between woman as lover and woman as mother. Psyche, violating Eros's prohibition, discovers that the stories she was told were based on false premises—Eros is not a monster nor in the end does he leave her. Jocasta enacts the story she was told with tragic consequences for herself as well as for others.

Jocasta's warning about the dangers of knowing mark her absence as a subject in this text. When the herdsman's tale reveals that it was she who gave him the child, the chorus comments to Oedipus on her silence:

O how have the furrows ploughed
by your father endured to bear you, poor wretch
and hold their peace for so long?[41]

Although the question: "Whose tale is more miserable [than Oedipus's]? Who is there lives with a savager fate?"[42] is unanswered, the answer implied is Jocasta—the unspeaking and in the end unspeakable mother.

Yet when she does speak of her own experience briefly before killing herself, she tries to make sense of what happened in what seemed a story of love:

> Do you remember, Laius, that night long past which bred a child
>   for us
> to send you to your death and leave a mother making children
>   with her son?[43]

Casting the night as the agent of action, she renders human connection a mystery and the story of abandonment comes full circle. Jocasta's tragedy consists in her failure twice to perceive the connection between mother and child or her inability in the context of this story to become a subject and perceiver in her own right. Consequently, she suffers for the most part in silence. Although her actions are central to this story of love, her silence becomes part of its mystery.

· · ·

The key to the riddle of femininity—that is, to the objectification of women and to women's silence—is the hidden figure of woman as both lover and mother in the story of love. It is the emergence of this figure as a perceiver and knower— that is, as a speaker rather than an object or mirror—that renders female development coherent and transforms the psychology of love. If women become known, then love becomes known as a matter of relationship, rather than a self-enclosed state. Told as a story involving two people—Eros and Psyche rather than Oedipus—it must be told from two different angles, as a joining of stories that depends on knowledge and thus on a language that gives access to people and feelings. Schneiderman points out that Oedipus's error in answering the riddle of the Sphinx was to generalize from his own state—to answer Man rather than Oedipus to this riddle about feet.[44] In *Love's Labour's Lost,* it is the separation of knowledge from common sense which guarantees that the King's academy will fail. Psychologists, casting women as objects and generalizing from men to human nature, make a similar mistake.[45] If women are a mystery, love is a mystery; and since the experience of relationships provides love's plain language, a gap enters the story that is covered over by romantic conventions or technical terms.

In retelling an old story of passionate attachment which is a story as well of female development, we have suggested that the problem of objectification is a problem of female adolescence—the time when beauty and sexuality render women objects of worship or of desire, the time when women encounter men's stories about love that impose a division between lovers and mothers, but also the time when girls gain the potential to become lovers and mothers themselves. The perception of this dual position of women in the story of love is essential for female development, since the figure of woman as mother and lover reveals the inescapable connection between women and women, as well as between women and men. As the story of Eros and Psyche demonstrates these connections in all their complications, leading them to be seen and in the end chosen, it reveals a story about love and passion that ends not in tragedy but with the birth of a child named Pleasure. In one sense more difficult, it is in the end a simpler story about love.

Epilogue
Passionate Attachments: The Essential but Fragile Nature of Love

ROBERT MICHELS

The need to explain love and other passionate attachments stems in part from the assumptions that are built into our language and our view of man. We often speak and think as though man were "naturally" devoid of passion; a creature alive and reactive but without strong feelings or emotions. From this perspective, passion is a state that intrudes on the natural condition, and therefore one that must be explained. Of course, this view tells us more about our own cultural bias than about the biology or psychology of the species. Cool, detached, unpassionate mental states may occur from time to time, but they are certainly the exception rather than the rule; and even when they seem to be present they are often merely screens that conceal hidden emotions. Indeed one of the central discoveries of psychoanalysis in the early part of this century was that passion was ubiquitous, and that when the surface appearance was tranquil, hidden passion could be discovered. Dreams, normal childhood, and many adult personality types could no longer be viewed as bland or innocent. Lust and rage were the norm, and if there was anything that still had to be questioned or explained, it was the occasional episode of mental activity that was relatively distant from hidden passions. Passion was no longer to be seen as an epiphenomenon, but rather a central feature of human psychology of immense adaptive significance, both to the individual and to the species.

Our attitude toward the concept of attachment is similar. We speak and think of individuals, persons, selves, and others, as though man were naturally separate or alone and it was social structures or attachments that required explanation. However, unlike many lower animals, humans cannot survive as solitary creatures. The prolonged helplessness of the newborn requires a protective community. The predisposition to social attachments is even reflected by human anatomy—genitalia, breasts, and the larynx are all rather inefficiently designed for life in social isolation. However, the myth of a "natural" state in which man is alone is a powerful one, reflected both in our political philosophy of social contracts and personal liberties and in our need to explain attachment as well as passion.

"Passion" and "attachment" are integrally related in their origins. The adaptive value of most passionate emotions, such as love, hate, or dependency, is based on their ability to energize attachments. The evolution of the capacity for emotion is intertwined with the role of social relationships in human biology and the importance of emotions as the motivational substrata for those relationships.

What does it mean to "discuss" or "explain" something that is so fundamental to the very nature of man? We can describe passionate attachments, their various forms at different stages of development, in men and women, in various cultures, and at different times in history. We can examine the inner meanings that are associated with them, the thoughts and fantasies, both conscious and unconscious, that are as much a part of the human condition as the behaviors that can be observed and described from the outside. We can trace the various secondary functions that these attachments come to serve in different settings—the economic, religious, social, or political arrangements that become aspects of passionate attachments and may even come to overwhelm and regulate the original psychobiological role of the attachment. Finally, we can study, and admire, the creative transformations of these passions into the works of art and literature that constitute our highest cultural achievements. In short, we can place passionate attachments in developmental, cultural, or historic contexts, we can isolate and examine their psychological, social, political or economic components, and we can wonder at the beauty of their symbols.

Several themes and problems appear repeatedly in thinking about love, the prototype of all passions. First, love is only one of the passions that can lead to attachment and it is often found in relationship to others. Aggression or rage, dependence and nurturance, and fear are all intense emotions that tie humans to each other. Are these all aspects of a single process, or are they independent forces that may interfere with each other, the components or contaminants of love? Psychological maturation seems to involve the progressive integration of several different kinds of passions, particularly love and hate, into coherent bonds in intimate relationships. For example, clinicians know that regardless of the apparent strength of their positive feelings, if couples are unable to get angry with each other, their relationship is likely to regress into pathology. In brief, while love may be the most characteristic basis of passionate attachments, its boundaries with other passions are blurred and it is often admixed with other emotions. There are several ways to understand this; it can be seen as the integration of several sometimes conflicting emotions, with the dominance of love marking the healthiest or most mature outcome; as the debasement of love by lower emotions; or simply as further evidence of the complexity of human behavior and the simplicity of our language and our theories.

In the papers in this volume, Gaylin sees a biologically programed nurturant concern for infants and children as the prototype of human love, with sexual attachments as a secondary theme. In contrast, Stone reminds us that although it may be a biological necessity, parental love can be so transformed by social and economic arrangements that it is easier to trace the history of child abuse or even infanticide than that of passionate parental affection for the young. Kernberg mentions the mother-child bond as a major precursor of adult love, but also emphasizes the importance of the capacity to integrate love with aggression in all sustained intimate relationships and in "normal polymorphous perverse sexuality." Viederman and Kernberg both discuss danger, fear, and the gulf that separates lovers from the rest of the world, as an essential theme of love. "Pure" love can be seen as an abstraction; we are reminded again and again of the many interlacing and even contradictory passions that are found together with real love.

A second recurrent theme in our thinking about love is the extent to which our understanding is determined by history and by culture. Biology is relatively stable, but the most stable feature of human personality is its biological predisposition to immense flexibility and plasticity, with underlying structures altered and transformed by culture. Which aspects of human love are built in to those underlying structures, which are shaped by the culture in which the experience occurs, and which reflect the culture of the observer, along with his prejudices, biases, and categories of observation? A modern production of Shakespeare's *Antony and Cleopatra* may tell us more about our view of love than about Shakespeare's, just as the work itself may tell us more about Elizabethan than Egyptian love.

In this volume, Gaylin reminds us of the several kinds of human experience recognized by the Greeks, and condensed into our single term "love." May traces the relative dominance of contradictory attitudes toward love in various cultures, and Stone asserts most definitively that our experiences of love may tell us little about how people in the past felt about their passionate attachments. Cavell discusses romantic love as it is expressed in works of art throughout history. Love is shaped by culture and society; the love we know in our personal worlds is just that, and it may tell us relatively little about love in other cultures or other eras.

A third theme in thinking about love is the difference between men and women. Most believe that there are important differences, although recent feminist writers have criticized the earlier prejudice that saw the male experience as the prototype, with the female as only a variant. Once differences are described, further questions emerge. Are they biological, developmental, or cultural in origin? Perhaps most basic, is it possible to formulate the issue in neutral terms, or are sexist implications inevitable in our questions as well as our answers? For example, Gilligan and Stern suggest that the traditional psychoanalytical perspective divorces love and sexuality from human relationships, and thus reflects a male point of view. Presumably they would find object relations models more feminine than earlier psychoanalytic theories. They stress the importance of women as the subject rather than the object of love, and suggest that attempts at "scientific" objectivity lead to a false mystification of both love and femininity. They further suggest that masculinity and male love are somehow less violated by the theme of blind or one-sided love, together with a beloved who is object without being subject. Some might wonder whether they are merely replacing male sexist prejudices with female sexist prejudices, without solving the quest for a neutral framework for discussing sexual differences. It is striking how little attention the other authors pay to the differences between the sexes. It is almost as though we have given up trying to talk about the theme that is probably of greatest interest in popular culture, perhaps fearing that anything that is said will serve more to reveal the author's prejudices than to clarify the subject. It is also possible that the traditional emphasis on the difference between men and women in their passionate attachments reflects a tradition with waning influence, and that we are increasingly likely to attribute sexual differences to historical or cultural determinants.

A fourth theme is the relationship between sex and love. We think of lust and love as so closely related that they are sometimes regarded as synonymous. However, in adolescence, and in many cultures and through much of history they have been only casually linked. Lust may exist without any real attachment, and in many pathologic conditions it is as closely bound to aggression as it is to love. Nevertheless, love and sex do seem to have a special tie. Interestingly, in this volume it is the theologian, May, who focuses on the link between them, while the psychologists and psychoanalysts seem to suggest that we have overemphasized their relationship. May bases his argument on biology; sex and parenthood are linked by a causal relationship more fundamental than the sharing of affiliative bonds; and the trivialization of sex ignores that basic fact. He argues that sex is good, important, special, even ecstatic. The others don't disagree, but they do emphasize that love is far more than lust, that although intimate ties and powerful emotions can be traced to sexual roots, they can be traced to other roots as well, and that while sex is a powerful chord, it is only one chord in the symphony of love. In brief, they suggest that like the difference in loving between men and women, we may have overemphasized the link between sex and love.

A fifth theme is the transformation of passionate attachments in the course of an individual's development. In a sense, one of the core discoveries of psychoanalysis is that passion dominates the mental life of infancy, and it is only after it has been muted, tamed, and integrated into more complex psychological structures that any other type of psychic experience is possible. In this perspective passionate experiences in adult life always have regressive meanings, and always involve the reawakening of infantile states. Psychoanalysis is interested in the taming and transformation of passion, in the ways in which symbols, ideas, and fantasies can shape and mold passions. Kernberg speaks of some of the universal fantasies that color passionate attachments, their developmental origins and variations, and emphasizes the identity of those themes that enhance the intensity of relationships and those that can invade and destroy them. Viederman speaks of the importance of illusion, unreality, and mystery, the space in which fantasy can unfold, if passion is to be maintained. He also discusses the vicissitudes of passion across the life cycle. Implicit in the recognition of the importance of fantasy in passion and the need for ambiguity, mystery, and uncertainty if passion is to unfold, is the recognition that adult human passion is a psychic phenomenon, different from animal or newborn human passion in that it involves more than a biological drive. It can be shaped and altered by thoughts and images; it is weaker, and therefore inherently more modifiable. Of course, it is the very fragility of passion that gives it its uniquely human characteristic, that makes it vulnerable to so many transformations, deviations, and disorders, and that leads to its special claim of interest to psychoanalysis.

A sixth and final theme is the significance of love for the experience of self, and the mystery of human experience. If humans are, uniquely, loving animals, then love is part of human essence. Viederman speaks most directly to this theme, describing passionate love as the "closest thing to ever elusive happiness" catalyzing the formation of a new self. For Gaylin it is part of the essential psychological equipment of the species; "The ultimate pleasure . . . is the pleasure of loving," and in fact loving transcends pleasure. For Cavell marriage provides the essential denial of cosmic isolation. For Stone and for May it provides a perspective on the values and forms of a culture; for Kernberg, the mature integration of the multiple themes of psychological development; and for Gilligan and Stern the key that unlocks the secret of that development. Man is a loving animal. All agree that love and passionate attachments are an essential theme of human psychology, for both men and women, across cultures, through history, and throughout the life cycle. Love relationships have many meanings and can appear in a variety of forms. The insistence that any one of their common themes—social, sexual, nurturant, economic, religious, sexist, psychopathologic, or other—are of necessity central robs love of its human complexity and mystery. One essential feature of love may be that there is more to it than we can comprehend.

Notes

CHAPTER 1. VIEDERMAN: THE NATURE OF PASSIONATE LOVE

1. Engel, G. and Schmale, A. (1967). Psychoanalytic Theory of Somatic Disorder: Conversion, Specificity and the Disease Onset Situation. *J. of Amer. Psychoanalytic Assn.* 15:344–65.
2. Oxford English Dictionary (1971).
3. Michels, R. (1971). Student Dissent. *J. of Amer. Psychoanalytic Assn.* 19:423–27.
4. Freud, S. (1953). Introductory Lectures. *Standard Edition: XV.*
5. Loewald, H. (1971). The Transference Neurosis: Comments on the Concept and the Phenomenon. *J. of Amer. Psychoanalytic Assn.* 19:55.
6. Michels. Student Dissert.
7. Benedek, T. (1977). Ambivalence, Passion and Love. *J. of Amer. Psychoanalytic Assn.* 25:53–80.
   Landauer, K. (1938). Affects, Passions and Temperament. *Int'l J. of Psychoanalysis* 19:388–415.
8. Kernberg, O. (1977). Boundaries and Structure in Love Relationships. *J. of Amer. Psychoanalytic Assn.* 25:81–114.
9. Frisch, M. (1965) *Gantenbein*. Trans. M. Bullock (London: Methuen), pp. 127–30.
10. Bergman, Ingmar. (1978). *The Marriage Scenarios* (New York: Pantheon).

CHAPTER 2. STONE: PASSIONATE ATTACHMENTS IN THE WEST

1. Darnton, R. *The Great Cat Massacre and other Episodes in French Cultural History* (New York: Basic Books, 1984), 4.
2. For further discussion of these issues, and references, see my book *The Family, Sex and Marriage in England 1500–1800* (New York: Harper & Row, 1977).
3. *Journal of Family History*, 8, 1983, p. 100.
4. Flandrin, J.-L. *Les Amours Paysannes* (XVI–XIX Siècles) (Paris: Gallimard, 1975).
5. The literature on infanticide (rare), infant abandonment, and early death by deliberate neglect or wet-nursing in Western Europe up to the nineteenth century is now enormous. See for example:

    de Mause, L. *The History of Childhood* (New York: Psychohistory Press, 1974).

    Delasselle, C., 'Les enfants abandonés à Paris au XVIII siécle,' *Annales E.C.S.*, 30, Jan.–Feb. 1975.

    Flandrin, J.-L. 'L'attitude devant le petit enfant . . . dans la Civilisation Occidentale,' in *Annales de Demographie Historique*, 1973.

    Sussman, G. D. *Selling Mother's Milk: the Wet-nursing Business in France 1715–1914* (Champaign: Univ. of Illinois Press, 1982).

    Medick, H. and D. W. Sabean, eds., *Interest and Emotion* (New York: Cambridge University Press, 1984), 91.

CHAPTER 4. GAYLIN: LOVE AND THE LIMITS OF INDIVIDUALISM

1. P. D. Williams, *The Spirit and Forms of Love* (New York: Harper & Row, 1968), 2.
2. For a fuller discussion, see Gaylin, W. *Feelings: Our Vital Signs* (New York: Harper & Row, 1979).
3. Dubos, R. *So Human An Animal* (New York: Charles Scribner, 1968).
4. Klaus, M. et al. "Maternal Behavior at the First Contact with Her Young," *Pediatrics* 46 (1970), pp. 187–192.
5. Freud, S. *Inhibitions, Symptoms and Anxieties,* Standard Ed. XX, pp. 139–40. (London: Hogarth Press, 1966).
6. Breuer and Freud, S. *Studies on Hysteria,* S.E. II; (London: Hogarth Press.)
7. Freud, S. *Three Essays on the Theory of Sexuality* In: S.E. VII, 125–243.
8. Freud, S. *Civilization and Its Discontents,* 1930. S.E. Vol. XXI.
9. Freud, S. *Totem and Taboo,* 1912. S.E. Vol. XIII.
10. For one pioneering discussion, see Erikson, E. H. *Identity and the Life Cycle* (New York: International U. Press, 1959).

11. Plato. *The Symposium,* ed. B. Jowett (New York: Tudor Publishing, 1956), 315–18.

12. Mendus, S. "Marital Faithfulness," *Philosophy* Vol. 59, 1984, pp. 248, 251.

13. Solovyov, V. in *The Meaning of Love,* trans. Blas, G. (London: Century Press, 1945), 22–23.

14. James, W. in *The Writings of William James,* ed. J. McDermott (New York: Random House, 1967), 618–19.

CHAPTER 5. KERNBERG: BETWEEN CONVENTIONALITY AND AGGRESSION

1. Freud, S. (1905). Three Essays on the Theory of Sexuality. In: *S.E.* VII:135–243 (London: Hogarth Press, 1953).

_____ (1910) A Special Type of Choice of Objects Made by Men. In: *S.E.* XI:163–175 (London: Hogarth Press, 1957).

_____ (1912) On the Universal Tendency to Debasement in the Sphere of Love (Contributions to the Psychology of Love, II). In: *S.E.* XI:178–190 (London: Hogarth Press, 1957).

_____ (1914). On Narcissism. In: *S.E.* XIV:69–102 (London: Hogarth Press, 1957).

_____ (1918). The Taboo of Virginity (Contributions to the Psychology of Love III). In: *S.E.* XI:192–208 (London: Hogarth Press, 1957).

_____ (1921). Group Psychology and the Analysis of the Ego. In: *S.E.* XVIII:67–143 (London: Hogarth Press, 1955).

_____ (1922). Some Neurotic Mechanisms in Jealousy, Paranoia and Homosexuality. In: *S.E.* XVIII:223–232 (London: Hogarth Press, 1955).

_____ (1923). The Ego and the Id. In: *S.E.* XIX:13–66 (London: Hogarth Press, 1961).

_____ (1924). The Dissolution of the Oedipus Complex. In: *S.E.* XIX:173–182, 1961.

_____ (1925). Some Psychical Consequences of the Anatomical Distinction Between the Sexes. In: *S.E.* XIX:243–258 (London: Hogarth Press, 1961).

2. Kernberg. (1976). *Object Relations Theory and Clinical Psychoanalysis* (New York: Aronson).

_____ (1980). *Internal World and External Reality* (New York: Aronson).

3. Freud. Special Type of Choice; Tendency to Debasement: Taboo of Virginity; Dissolution of the Oedipus Complex.

4. Bergmann, M. S. (1982). Platonic Love, Transference Love, and Love in Real Life. In: *J. of Amer. Psychoanalytic Assn.* 30:87–111.

5. Braunschweig, D. and Fain, M. (1971). *Eros et Anteros* (Paris: Petite Bibliotheque Payot).

6. Chasseguet-Smirgel, J. (1970). *Female Sexuality* (Ann Arbor: Univ. of Michigan Press).
   Kernberg. *Object Relations Theory; Internal World.*
   Blum, H. P. (1976). Masochism, the Ego Ideal, and the Psychology of Women. *J. of the Amer. Psychoanalytic Assn.* 24 (suppl.): 157–191.

7. Chasseguet-Smirgel. (1974). Perversion, Idealisation and Sublimation. *Int'l J. of Psycho-Analysis.* 55:349–357.

8. Bergman. (1971). Psychoanalytic Observations on the Capacity to Love. In: *Separation-Individuation,* eds. J. B. McDevitt and C. F. Settlage (New York: Int'l Univ. Press), 15–40.
   Mahler, M. S. (1968). *On Human Symbiosis and the Vicissitudes of Individuation. Vol. 1: Infantile Psychosis* (New York: Int'l Univ. Press).

9. Fairbairn, W. D. (1952). *An Object-Relations Theory of the Personality* (New York: Basic Books).
   Klein, M. (1945). The Oedipus Complex in the Light of Early Anxieties. In: *Contributions to Psycho-Analysis, 1921–1945* (London: Hogarth Press, 1948), 377–390.
   Mahler, *Human Symbiosis.*
   Jacobson, E. (1964). *The Self and the Object World* (New York: Int'l Univ. Press).

10. Kernberg. *Object Relations Theory,* and *Internal World.*

11. Klein. (1949). Early States of the Oedipus Conflict and of Superego Formation. In: *The Psycho-Analysis of Children* (London: Hogarth Press), 179.
    Jacobson. *Self and the Object World.*
    Blum. Masochism.
    Chasseguet-Smirgel. (1985). *The Ego Ideal* (New York: Norton).

12. Klein. Oedipus Conflict and Superego Formation.
    Jacobson. *Self and the Object World.*
    Blum. Masochism.

13. Dicks, H. V. (1967). *Marital Tensions* (New York: Basic Books).

14. Chasseguet-Smirgel. (1984). *Creativity and Perversion* (New York: Norton).

15. Braunschweig and Fain. *Eros et Anteros.*

16. Turquet, P. (1975). Threats to Identity in the Large Group. In: *The Large Group: Dynamics and Therapy,* ed. L. Kreeger (London: Constable), 87–144.

CHAPTER 7. GILLIGAN AND STERN: THE RIDDLE OF FEMINITY AND THE PSYCHOLOGY OF LOVE

1. William Shakespeare, *Love's Labour Lost,* I.i. 56–57, in *The Riverside Shakespeare,* G. Blakemore Evans, ed. (Boston: Houghton Mifflin, 1974).

2. *Ibid.,* I.i. 80–83.

3. *Ibid.,* V.ii. 861–63.

4. *Ibid.,* V.ii. 469.

5. *Ibid.,* V.ii. 753.

6. *Ibid.,* V.ii. 412–13.

7. Sigmund Freud, *Three Essays on the Theory of Sexuality* (1905), in *Standard Edition* VII, James Strachey, ed. and trans. (London: Hogarth Press, 1961), p. 151.

8. Bruno Bettelheim, *The Uses of Enchantment: The Meaning and Importance of Fairy Tales* (New York: Vintage, 1977), p. 292.

9. Erich Neumann, *Amor and Psyche: The Psychic Development of the Feminine* (Princeton: Bollingen, 1956); Bettelheim, *Uses of Enchantment;* Lee Edwards, *Psyche as Hero* (Middletown, Conn: Wesleyan University Press, 1984), p. 12.

10. Bettelheim, *Uses of Enchantment,* p. 295.

11. Edwards, *Psyche as Hero,* p. 11.

12. Neuman, *Amor and Psyche,* pp. 83, 139.

13. Apuleius, *The Golden Ass,* W. Adlington, trans. (Cambridge: Loeb Classical Library, 1915), p. 193.

14. *Ibid.,* p. 197.

15. *Ibid.*

16. *Ibid.,* p. 193.

17. *Ibid.,* p. 199.

18. *Ibid.,* p. 205.

19. *Ibid.,* p. 207.

20. *Ibid.*

21. *Ibid.,* p. 219.

22. *Ibid.,* p. 221.

23. *Ibid.*, p. 231.
24. *Ibid.*, p. 233.
25. *Ibid.*, p. 237.
26. *Ibid.*, p. 279.
27. Neumann, *Amor and Psyche*, p. 125.
28. Bettelheim, *Uses of Enchantment*, p. 292.
29. Edwards, *Psyche as Hero*, p. 12.
30. Apuleius, *The Golden Ass*, p. 279.
31. *Ibid.*, p. 241.
32. *Ibid.*, p. 235.
33. *Ibid.*, pp. 279, 281.
34. Neumann, *Amor and Psyche*, p. 84.
35. Bruno Bettelheim, *Freud and Man's Soul* (New York: Vintage, 1984), p. 11.
36. *Ibid.*, pp. 11–12.
37. *Ibid.*, p. 12.
38. Freud, *The Question of Lay Analysis* (1926), in *Standard Edition* XX (1961), p. 212.
39. Freud, *Feminity* (1933), Lecture XXXIII, *New Introductory Lectures on Psychoanalysis*, in *Standard Edition* XXII (1961), pp. 116, 135.
40. Freud, *Three Essays on the Theory of Sexuality*, p. 222.
41. Sophocles, *Oedipus Rex*, in *Greek Tragedies*, David Grene, trans., David Grene and Richmond Lattimore, eds. (Chicago: University of Chicago Press, 1960), vol. 1, p. 164.
42. *Ibid.*
43. *Ibid.*, p. 166.
44. Stuart Schneiderman, *Jacques Lacan: The Death of an Intellectual Hero* (Cambridge: Harvard University Press, 1983), p. 82.

Index

Abstinence, 28–29
Adam's Rib, 89–90
Adolescent groups, 80, 82
Adultery, 17
Agape, 42
Aggression, 65–71, 74–76, 79–83, 117, 118
Allen, Woody, 8
Ambivalence, tolerance of, 70
Antony and Cleopatra (Shakespeare), 89, 90, 93, 118
Apuleius, 104
Aristophanes, myth of, 56–57
Aristotle, xii, 61
Arthur, Jean, 93
Aucassin and Nicolette, story of, 17
Auden, W. H., 32

Battering parents, 55
Benedek, T., 4
Bergman, Ingmar, 6
Bergmann, M. S., 66, 69
Bettelheim, Bruno, 104, 105, 109, 111
Bisexuality, 64, 66
Blum, H. P., 74
Body-representation, 9
Braunschweig, D., 67, 68
Breuer, Josef, 50
Brief Encounter (Coward), 29
Bundling, 21–22
Burn-out, 12

Calvinism, 25
Capra, Frank, 93, 95
Caring emotions, 48–53
Cartland, Barbara, 88
Castration, 37
  anxiety, 66, 74

Casual attitude to sex, 27, 32–34, 36–37
Cavell, Stanley, 85–100, 118, 121
Chasseguet-Smirgel, J., 68, 75, 79
Child abuse, 25, 117
Chivalry, 6
Circumcision, 37
Civilization and Its Discontents (Freud), x, 51–52
Commitment, 59–61
Community, xii, 52, 58, 60
Conscience, 52, 54
Cooper, Gary, 93
Countertransference, 64
Coward, Noel, 29
Cupid and Psyche, myth of, 104–114

Danger, 8–9, 118
Darnton, Robert, 15
Davis, Bette, 93, 95–97
De Rougemont, Denis, 29, 34, 87, 90
Declaration of Independence, 19
Demonic, sex as, 27, 28–31, 37–38
Dependency, xii, 48–50, 117
Depression, 53, 54
Descartes, René, 91, 92
Devil's Share, The (De Rougemont), 34
Dialectic of Sex, The (Firestone), 86
Dicks, H. V., 75–76
Direct triangulation, 71–73, 75, 79
Discipline, 37–38
Disgust, 51

Distance, 7, 13, 29
Distance receptors, 46–47
Divine, sex as, 27, 31–32, 38
Divorce, 18, 21, 92
Dostoevsky, Fëdor, 39
Dubois, Rene, 49

Edwards, Lee, 105, 109
Ego-defense mechanisms, 51
"Ego and the Id, The" (Freud), 73
Ego ideal, xi, 10, 74–76
"Ego Ideal" (Chasseguet-Smirgel), 75
Emerson, Ralph Waldo, 91
Emotions
  caring, 48–53
  distinguished from sensations, 46–47
Engel, G., 1
Epithemia, 41
Eros, 41
Eros and Anteros (Braunschweig and Fain), 68
Eros and Psyche, myth of, 104–114
Erotomania, 13
"Essays on the Understanding of Love" (Freud), 53
Exhibitionism, 64, 65
Extra-uterine life, 48–49

Fain, M., 67, 68
Fairbairn, W. D., 70
Family, xii, 20–21
Fantasy, 13, 71–72, 120
Fear, 47, 53, 117, 118
Female Eunuch, The (Greer), 86
Femininity, riddle of, 101–114, 119

Feminist movement, x, 33
Ferenczi, Sandor, 4
Filia, 41–42
Films, 88–90, 92–100
Firestone, Shulamith, 86
Fonda, Henry, 88
For Whom the Bell Tolls (Hemingway), 38
Forster, E. M., 85
Foundling hospitals, 24
Freud, Sigmund, x–xii, 4, 19, 43, 49, 55, 63, 89, 93, 103
  groups and, 52, 78
  identification and, 54, 56
  infantile sexuality and, 64, 66
  libido theory and, xi, 44–45, 51, 53
  neurosis theory and, 43, 50
  Oedipus complex and, 66–68, 74, 112
  psychoanalysis, introduction of term, 111
  repression and, 51
  superego and, 54, 73
  transference and, 99
Freud and Man's Soul (Bettelheim), 111
Frisch, Max, 5–6, 11
Fusion, 54, 56–57, 61, 69

Gantebein (Frisch), 5–6, 11
Gaylin, Willard, 41–62, 117, 118, 121
Gender revolution, 55
Gilligan, Carol, 101–114, 119, 121
Gorer, Geoffrey, 30
Gradiva (Jensen), 93

Greer, Germaine, 86
"Group Psychology and the Analysis of the Ego" (Freud), 75, 78
Groups, 52, 78–80
Guilt, 2, 47, 48, 53, 75–77

Hate, 117
Hawthorne, Nathaniel, 91, 92, 98
Hefner, Hugh, 36
Helmholz, Hermann, xi
Hemingway, Ernest, 38
Henreid, Paul, 93, 95, 96
Homosexuality, 64, 65
Hume, David, 91

Identification, 54, 56, 61
Illegitimacy, 19, 60
Illusion, 7, 10, 11, 14, 120
Imagination, 55
Incest, 67, 74, 79
Individualism, 20, 26, 58, 59
Infancy, xii, 48–50, 57–58, 116, 120
Infant mortality, 24
Infanticide, 23–25, 117
Infantile sexuality, 64–66, 80
Inhibitions, Symptoms and Anxiety (Freud), 50
Internal World and External Reality (Kernberg), 69, 78
Interpretation of Dreams, The (Freud), 112
Introjection, 54, 74
Issac, Glynn, ix

Jacobson, E., 70, 74
James, William, 61–62

Japan, divorce in, 18
Jealousy, 8, 71, 73, 76, 77
Jefferson, Thomas, 19
Jensen, Wilhelm, 93
Jocasta, 112–113

Kant, Immanuel, 91
Kernberg, Otto F., 4, 63–83, 118, 120, 121
"Kitsch" art, 81
Klaus, M., 49
Klein, M., 70, 74

Lady Chatterley's Lover (Lawrence), 31–32
Lady Eve, The, 88
Landauer, K., 4
Landers, Ann, 34–35
Language of love, 102–103
Latency groups, 80, 82
Lawrence, D. H., 31–32, 33, 38
Libertinism, 80–82
Libido theory, xi, xiii, 43–45, 51, 53, 59
Loathing, 51
Locke, John, 92
Loewald, H., 4
Love: *see* Marriage; Passionate love; Romantic love; Sexuality
Love Story (Segal), 29
Love in the Western World (De Rougemont), 87
Love's Labour's Lost (Shakespeare), 101–102, 113

Mahler, M. S., 69, 70
Manichaeanism, 28–29, 31, 35, 37–38

Marriage, xii, 120
  bourgeois view of, 30
  changing relationship of pas-
    sionate love to, 20
  in 18th century, 18
  expectations in, 38–39
  Manichaean view of, 28
  romantic, 85–100
  sentimental view of, 32
  in 16th century, 17–18
  "trial," 60
Masochism, 64, 65, 71, 77
Mastery, 9
Matricide, 66, 67
May, William F., 27–39, 118–
    121
Medieval romance, 7, 13
Mendus, Susan, 60
Michels, Robert, 3, 4, 115–121
Middle age, passionate love
    and, 12
Milton, John, 92
Mr. Deeds Goes to Town, 93–95
Mitchell, Juliet, 86–88, 90, 97
Morality, 79–82
Mother-child relationship, xi,
    49, 64, 117–118
  history of, 23–26
Mystery, 4, 7–8, 13, 14, 104,
    110–113, 119–121

Narcissism, 65, 68, 69
Neoplatonists, 42
Neumann, Erich, 105, 109
Neurosis, 43, 50
No Sex, Please. We're British, 34
Novels, xii, 19, 20, 88, 104
Now Voyager, 93, 95–99
Nuisance, sex as a, 27, 34–35,
    37

Objectification, 103, 106–110,
    113–114, 119
"Observations on Transfer-
    ence-Love" (Freud), 99
Oedipus complex, x, 66–73, 74,
    112–113

Pain, 13, 44–46, 59
Paradise Lost (Milton), 92
Parfit, Derek, 60
Parricide, 66, 67, 73, 79
Passionate love, 1–14, 117–121;
    see also Romantic love;
    Sexuality
  attributes and psychodynam-
    ics of, 5–14
  definitions, 2–3
  psychoanalytic literature on, 4
Penis envy, 68, 69, 74
Perversions, 64, 65
Plato, 56–57, 103
Platonic love, 42
Pleasure, 43–46, 53, 58–62
Poe, Edgar Allan, 91
Pornography, 30, 77–78
"Pornography of Death, The"
    (Gorer), 30
Pride, 47
Printing, invention of, 17
Projection, 74
Psychoanalysis and Feminism
    (Mitchell), 86
Pulp fiction, 19, 88
Puritanism, 32, 80–82
Pursuits of Happiness (Cavell),
    90, 92

Rage, 47, 53, 117
Rains, Claude, 93, 95
Repression, 51

Responsibility, 59, 60
Reverse triangulation, 71–73, 75, 79
Robbins, Denise, 88
Romantic love, xi–xiii; *see also* Passionate love; Sexuality
  dualism in, 29
  history of, 16–22
  marriage and, 85–100
  relationship of passion to, 6–7
Rousseau, Jean-Jacques, 25

Sadism, 64, 65
St. Augustine, 38
Scenes from a Marriage, 6
Schmale, A., 1
Schneiderman, Stuart, 113
Second Treatise of Government (Locke), 92
Self-actualization movements, 60
Self-representation, 9–10, 13, 14, 70
Separation-individuation, stage of, 70
Sex therapy, 76
Sexual revolution, x, 60, 81
Sexuality, 19, 20–22, 119–120
  casual sex, 27, 32–34, 36–37
  demonic, sex as, 27, 28–31, 37–38
  divine, sex as, 27, 31–32, 38
  fantasies, 71–72, 120
  infantile, 64–66, 80
  libido theory, xi, xiii, 43–45, 51, 53, 59
  nuisance, sex as, 27, 34–35, 37

Oedipus complex, x, 66–73, 74, 112–113
  pleasure principle, 43–45
Shakespeare, William, 17, 24, 29, 89, 90, 93, 101–102, 113, 118
Shame, 51
Skepticism, 91
Socrates, 56, 102
Solovyov, Vladimir, 61
"Some Psychical Consequences of the Anatomical Distinction Between the Sexes" (Freud), 74
Song of Solomon, 29
"Special Type of Choice of Objects Made by Men, A" (Freud), 67
Stanwyck, Barbara, 88
Stern, Eve, 101–114, 119, 121
Stone, Lawrence, 15–26, 117, 118, 121
Studies of Hysteria (Freud and Breuer), 50
Sturges, Preston, 88
Suffering, 2
Sufi tradition, xii
Superego, 54, 56, 73–77
Swaddling, 23
Symbiosis, stage of, 70
Symposium (Plato), 56–57

Teenage pregnancy, 60
Ten Commandments, 79
"Tendency to Debasement in Love, The" (Freud), 89
"Theme of the Three Caskets, The" (Freud), 112
Thoreau, Henry David, 91

"Three Essays on the Theory of Sexuality" (Freud), 64, 66, 68, 111
Totem and Taboo (Freud), 52
Transference, 2, 4, 54, 66–67, 99
Transgression, 8–10, 14
Tristan and Iseult, myth of, 29
Troubadours, 17
Two Cheers for Democracy (Forster), 85

Unconscious, 50
Unconsummation, 13, 17
Uncontrollability, 3

Values, 56
Victorians, 27, 28, 56
Viederman, Milton, 1–14, 118, 120, 121
Violence, 30–31; *see also* Aggression
Voyeurism, 64, 65

Wet-nursing, 23–24, 26
Williams, Daniel, 41
Wishfulness, 7
Women: The Longest Revolution (Mitchell), 86
Women writers, 104, 118–119
Women's movement, x, 33
Wundt, Wilhelm, xi